The Atlas of
WOMEN

new revised third edition

Joni Seager teaches geography and women's studies at the University of Vermont. She is also a co-director in a Boston-based project to develop the Center for New Words, an organization committed to the empowerment of diverse women's and girls' writing and ideas. She has written widely on international environmental and women's issues. Her other books include *Earth Follies: Coming to Feminist Terms with the Global Environmental Crisis*; two editions of *The State of the Environment Atlas*; and *Putting Women in Place: Feminist Geographies*.

The Atlas of Women "is the innovative atlas no thoughtful person, male or female, should be without. Using maps and graphics, the authors present the worldwide condition of women. The material is coolly statistical or geographical; the aim is facts, not a manifesto. A wealth of facsinating information."
— *Washington Post*

"a fascinating atlas ... A compilation of facts about women's status, work, health, education, and personal freedom across the globe, it is not only an invaluable reference book, but also throws up questions about why a woman's lot is not as good as a man's." — *The Independent*

"a major reference tool...the atlas format and highly original and colorful statistical illustrations make this book as enjoyable as it is important. Highly recommended for school, public and academic libraries." — *Library Journal*

"an appealing idea, imaginatively executed"
— *Times Educational Supplement*

"packed full of fascinating and surprising nuggets of information... Like all the best fun books, this atlas has a serious point." — *New Internationalist*

" ... wonderful! It focuses on the right areas, asks the right questions; and the answers to those questions are instantly available because of the format. Even those who prefer to ignore or dismiss "women's issues" (which are, of course, general human issues) should feel shame when they spot on a chart their own country's low performance in an area."
— Marilyn French

"An imaginative, useful book...unlike anything I've ever seen.
Also fun to use."
— Alice Walker

"An excellent achievement: women's global status at a glance."
— Dale Spender

"Joni Seager's atlas is scholarly, funny, provocative
and an essential resource in any library.
You can't teach global issues without it. "
— Diane Bell, Professor of Anthropology,
George Washington University

"In this era of globalization
we are in desperate need of accurate information
that demonstrates how crucial
women are to the whole process... This atlas does just that.
Congratulations: Joni Seager has done it again!"
— Kum-Kum Bhavnani
Professor of Sociology, University of California at Santa Barbara

"Cheers for updating Seager's *Women in the World* !
The clear presentation of information
about women from around the world
 have made earlier versions among the
most useful resources for all Women's Studies courses."
— Claire G. Moses, Professor of Women's Studies,
University of Maryland

The Atlas of
WOMEN

new revised third edition

Joni Seager

First published in Great Britain by
The Women's Press Ltd, 2003
A member of the Namara Group
34 Great Sutton Street, London EC1V 0LQ

A catalogue record for this book is available from the British
Library

ISBN: 0 7043 4759 8

Produced for The Women's Press by
Myriad Editions Limited
6–7 Old Steine, Brighton BN1 1EJ, UK
http://www.MyriadEditions.com

Edited and co-ordinated for Myriad Editions by
Candida Lacey and Jannet King
Design and graphics by Corinne Pearlman and Isabelle Lewis
Cartography by Isabelle Lewis

Printed and bound in Hong Kong
under the supervision of Bob Cassels,
The Hanway Press, London

Contents

for Cynthia

and in memory of Anne Benewick

Introduction

There have been some remarkable improvements in the state of women since the first edition of this atlas was published in 1986. Improvements in women and girls' literacy and education top the list of global success stories; women have won voting rights and the right to hold public office in all but a small handful of countries; most of the world's governments have signed international treaties committed to women's rights. The importance of such gains should not be underestimated.

But, overall, the "success story" list is depressingly short. Many women around the world have experienced an absolute decline in the quality of their life over the past decade. Improvements in one place are not necessarily transferable to other places: we remain a world divided. The globalizing new world economy is based largely on exploiting "flexible" markets of underpaid workers; women's participation in this new world economy is not an unalloyed sign of progress. The global gap between rich and poor has widened, and there are now more women and men living in dire poverty than a decade ago; women remain the poorest of the poor, everywhere. Around the world, "structural adjustment" policies coordinated and imposed by rich-world governments have plunged country after country into social and economic crisis; it is women who have borne the cost of managing the economic fallout. Wars have wracked several countries; in Afghanistan, Bosnia, Chechnya, and Rwanda (among others) millions of people are living under wrenching conditions. Women bear a special burden of these wars, including horrific mass rapes, erosion of their rights, and the unrelenting demands of sustaining families and households in the midst of chaos. In former socialist countries, women are paying an especially high price for the transition to a free-market economy and society: everywhere this transition brings with it skyrocketing rates of violence and sexual exploitation, sharp increases in women's unemployment, an abrupt end to government support for healthcare, childcare, and housing, and even less representation for women in the emerging economic and political elites than they had in the old regimes. Religious fundamentalism and a resurgent conservative intolerance threaten women's rights in a wide range of states – and in a wide range of ways – across the globe. Millions of women around the world live their daily lives as little more than chattels. Large-scale systems of enslavement and oppression of women, including, prominently, sex trafficking, are flourishing.

Where is the outrage? Women do not automatically share in broad social advances: a rising tide does not necessarily raise all boats unless there is a commitment to do so. Feminists have often warned that gains in women's empowerment should not be taken for granted: they are fragile and reversible and always under pressure. This warning has never been more pertinent. At best we can say that from Pakistan to the USA, from Russia to Sierra Leone, the halls and hallmarks of power remain remarkably unperturbed by the oppression of women. At worst, evidence suggests that a remarkable number of governments in 2002 seem committed to turning back advances in women's autonomy.

Feminist organizing is stronger, more diverse, and more skilled than ever. International feminist networks have broken the isolation of women from one another; feminists everywhere are more informed about issues and perspectives from cultures and places outside their own immediate realm. Global feminist organizing is successfully redefining "human rights" to incorporate a broad agenda of "women's rights." Lesbian organizing has come out of the closet. As we enter the 21st century, we need public and civic leaders who will build on these feminist foundations to make unflinching real – not rhetorical – commitments to social justice for women.

As a feminist, I believe that social analysis and activism can be enriched by an international and broadly comparative perspective. However, working at a global scale also inevitably entails a degree of generalization that is troubling – and, indeed, that if left unexamined can undermine feminist analysis. The world of women is defined both by commonality and difference. Women everywhere share primary responsibility for having and rearing children, for forming and maintaining families, for contraception. They share too the lead in fighting for women's rights and other civil rights. Rich and poor, they also suffer rape, health traumas from illegal abortions, the degradation of pornography. Nonetheless, if we have learned anything from the feminist movement of the past three decades, it is that global generalizations must not be used to mask the very real differences that exist among women country by country, region by region. There are significant inequalities in wealth and in access to opportunities from place to place; these are then refracted and magnified by social signifiers such as race, ethnicity, age, or religious affiliation.

It is as a geographer that I have found a way to strike a balance between the demands of acknowledging both commonality and difference: at its best, mapping can simultaneously illuminate both. Mapping is a powerful tool; in showing not only what is happening but where, patterns are revealed on maps that would never be apparent in statistical tables or even in narratives. The similarities and differences, the continuities and contrasts among women around the world are perhaps best shown by mapping out – literally – their lives. It is my hope that this atlas raises as many questions as it provides answers.

There are many people without whom this atlas would not have been completed – or even started:

As always, I owe special thanks to my partner Cynthia Enloe, who never ceases to impress me with her analytical grasp, her intellectual generosity, and her amazing files of newspaper clippings; without Cynthia's encouragement and support I would not be able to imagine doing this atlas. The team at Myriad Editions, Candida Lacey, Isabelle Lewis, Jannet King and Corinne Pearlman, performed astounding creative, editorial, and production feats to bring this project to fruition. I miss the friendship and inspiration of Anne Benewick, the founder of Myriad; I wouldn't have arrived here at the third edition without her companionship on the journeys of the first and second. Special thanks and credit to Annie Olson, co-originator and co-author of the first edition. My family – Joan, Jade, John, Jody, Brad, Angie, Jeremy, Robin, Jackie, Julie, Stefan, Kim, Kris, and the newest generations of Bean, Natasha, Aidan and Jonathan – are a constant source of support and entertainment. To Gilda Bruckman and Judy Wachs, my extended family, I owe great debt and thanks. This atlas was further sustained by wide networks of friends and colleagues who brought me friendship, data, encouragement, and advice. Among them, my thanks especially to: Julie Abraham, Diane Bell, Alison Bernstein, Ellen Cooney, Mona Domosh, Madeline Drexler, Glen Elder, EJ Graff, Matthew Hannah, Sandra Harding, Jane Knodell, Amy Lang, Emma Lang, Wendy Luttrell, Mikaela Luttrell-Rowland, Stephanie Seguino, Robert Shreefter, Emma Shreefter, Joan Smith, Ellen Winchester, Laura Zimmerman; thanks also to my colleagues in the Committee on Women, Population and Environment, at New Words and the Center for New Words, and in the Geography and Women's Studies departments at the University of Vermont.

My thanks to Victoria Lane, who provided professional research assistance and encouragement on several maps; her colleagues in librarianship, Debra Farrey, Donna Thompson, and Charlie Irwin, provided outstanding research support for several maps. Additionally, many people provided data for particular research inquiries: Evelyn Murphy, Brandeis

University; Frances Sheahan, Interrights; Felicity Hill, UNIFEM; Judy Norsigian, Boston Women's Health Book Collective; Marlene Fried, Hampshire College; Isis Nusair, Clark University; Lori Manning, WREI; Aaron Belkin, Center for the Study of Sexual Minorities in the Military; Nooreddin Azimi, Guilan University, Iran; Vijaya Joshi, Clark University; Sophia Huyer, Women in Global Science and Technology; Amrita Basu, Amherst College; Gregory Gause, University of Vermont; Dyan Mazurana, University of Montana. Despite the best advice and assistance of all these people, I am sure that I have committed errors both of omission and commission; for these, I apologize and claim sole responsibility.

Beyond these particular acknowledgements, I have never lost sight of the broader social and intellectual debt that I owe to the countless feminists – most unnamed and unrecognized – who, for years and often at great personal cost, have been the only ones insisting that it is important to ask questions about where the women are. Without the collective support of women's movements around the globe, and the pathbreaking efforts of a persistent few, I would have neither the knowledge nor the confidence to undertake this atlas.

Joni Seager
Somerville, Massachusetts
November 2002

Part One
WOMEN IN THE WORLD

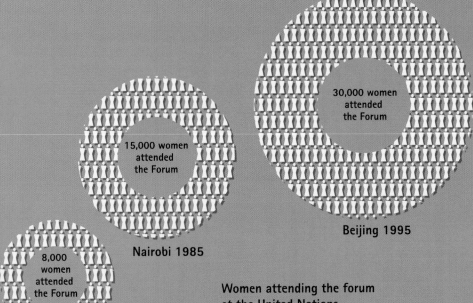

30,000 women
attended
the Forum

Beijing 1995

15,000 women
attended
the Forum

Nairobi 1985

8,000
women
attended
the Forum

Copenhagen 1980

**Women attending the forum
at the United Nations
World Conferences on Women**
1975 to 1995

6,000
women
attended
the Forum

Mexico 1975

**Governments sending official delegations
to the United Nations
World Conferences on Women**
1975 to 1995

133 governments	145 governments	157 governments	189 governments
Mexico 1975	Copenhagen 1980	Nairobi 1985	Beijing 1995

11

Gender-related development

Changes in GDI rank
1995–2000

2000 rank	1995 rank
increase	*decrease*
from 1995	*from 1995*

1995 rank	2000 rank
	1
2	
Belgium	Australia
	9	8
14	New Zealand
17	
	18
Ireland	25
27	Czech Republic
	32
	40
43	
Venezuela	Thailand
57	
	60
66	
Ukraine	72
76	74
Uzbekistan	77	83
86	China	South Africa
	93	88
	Saudi Arabia
97	102
Nicaragua	
105	
109	
115	India	Cambodia	115
	Cameroon
	124
128	129

There is no easy way to compare the status of women around the world. Indeed, it is unwise to attempt to use any single lens through which to do so.

Nonetheless, there are ways of shedding some light on women's status and quality of life. The Gender Development Index (GDI) provides one such surrogate measure. Developed by the United Nations Development Programme, the GDI ranks countries according to a set of basic "quality of life" measures, such as literacy and income, which are then adjusted according to the degree of gender disparity in each measure. One of the points illustrated by the GDI is that gender equality can be largely affected by an intentional commitment to equality principles and policies. For example, Scandinavian countries, which have adopted gender equality and women's empowerment as conscious

national policies, rank very high in the GDI index.

GDI values for almost all countries have improved over the past three decades, but the pace of progress has been uneven. Each year some countries slip significantly in rank, while others improve. Although a drop in rank does not necessarily mean conditions for women in that country have deteriorated, it does mean that the pace of progress has been slower than elsewhere.

Gender Development Index

2000
The GDI is based on key development indicators, including life expectancy, educational attainment, and income.

- top 10 countries
  least disparity between men and women
- high rank
- medium rank
- low rank
- bottom 10 countries
  most disparity between men and women
- no data

- life expectancy for women is under 55 years
  age given

As a broad political observation, we might say that women everywhere face *de facto* restrictions on their public presence, dress, and private and public behavior. But in many countries, "keeping women in their place" is a literal undertaking. Mobility and dress restrictions, enforced in a surprising number of countries, are rooted in standard patriarchal assumptions about men's right to control women, in potent combination with fundamentalist religious interpretations.

Women's rights are under increasing pressure from religious fundamentalism in many countries – Hindu fundamentalism in India, Christian fundamentalism in the USA, Roman Catholic fundamentalism in Croatia, Islamic fundamentalism in Algeria, among others. The rising tide of fundamentalism is everywhere contested. Feminists have been especially active in challenging the legitimacy of fundamentalist proscriptions, and in offering alternative interpretations of religious texts.

Restrictions on women are in most cases symptomatic of wider human rights abuses and political repression. They are cultivated in a climate of widespread oppression that affects women and men in many ways.

UNITED STATES
OF AMERICA

USA: State legislatures enacted 301 anti-abortion measures between 1995 and 2001; 86% of all US counties are now not served by an abortion provider.

VENEZUELA

Venezuela: A provision in the penal code provides that an adult man guilty of raping an adult woman with whom he is acquainted can avoid punishment if, before sentencing, he marries her.

The Practice of Purdah

seclusion of women is known to be an accepted practice *2002*

Women are restricted in their public movements, and often strictly cloistered in the home. In many of these countries, seclusion is practiced only among some ethnic or religious groups.

TUNISIA
MOROCCO
IRAN
AFGHANISTAN
KUWAIT
PAKISTAN
BAHRAIN
QATAR
UAE
OMAN
SAUDI ARABIA
BANGLADESH
INDIA
NIGER
especially among
Hausa and Fulani
ERITREA   YEMEN
NIGERIA
(Northern)
DJIBOUTI
CAMEROON
(Northern)
widely practiced

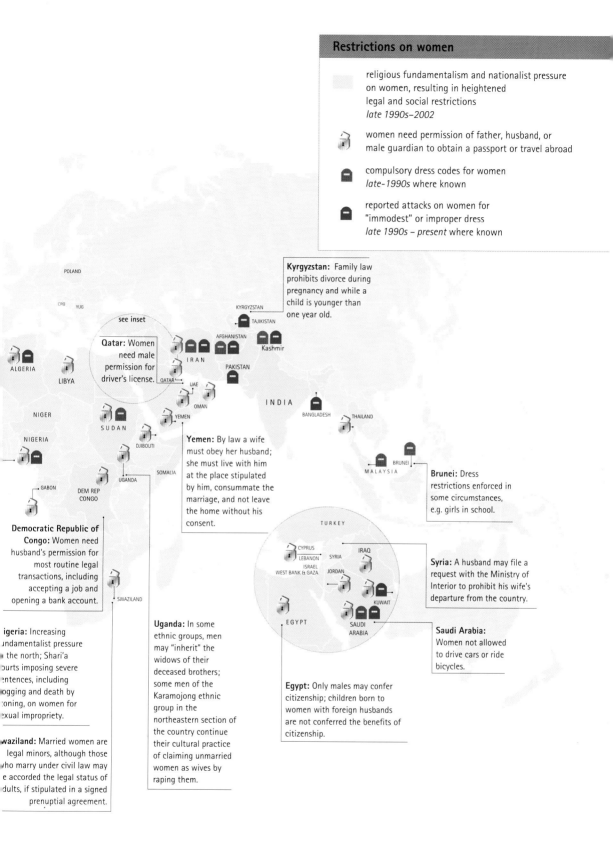

religious fundamentalism and nationalist pressure on women, resulting in heightened legal and social restrictions
late 1990s–2002

women need permission of father, husband, or male guardian to obtain a passport or travel abroad

compulsory dress codes for women
late-1990s where known

reported attacks on women for "immodest" or improper dress
late 1990s – present where known

POLAND

CRO   YUG

see inset

KYRGYZSTAN

TAJIKISTAN

AFGHANISTAN

Kashmir

Kyrgyzstan: Family law prohibits divorce during pregnancy and while a child is younger than one year old.

Qatar: Women need male permission for driver's license.

IRAN

QATAR   UAE

PAKISTAN

OMAN

INDIA

YEMEN

BANGLADESH   THAILAND

ALGERIA

LIBYA

NIGER

SUDAN

NIGERIA

DJIBOUTI

SOMALIA

UGANDA

GABON

DEM REP CONGO

Yemen: By law a wife must obey her husband; she must live with him at the place stipulated by him, consummate the marriage, and not leave the home without his consent.

MALAYSIA   BRUNEI

Brunei: Dress restrictions enforced in some circumstances, e.g. girls in school.

TURKEY

CYPRUS
LEBANON   SYRIA   IRAQ
ISRAEL
WEST BANK & GAZA   JORDAN

KUWAIT

EGYPT

SAUDI ARABIA

Syria: A husband may file a request with the Ministry of Interior to prohibit his wife's departure from the country.

Democratic Republic of Congo: Women need husband's permission for most routine legal transactions, including accepting a job and opening a bank account.

SWAZILAND

Uganda: In some ethnic groups, men may "inherit" the widows of their deceased brothers; some men of the Karamojong ethnic group in the northeastern section of the country continue their cultural practice of claiming unmarried women as wives by raping them.

Saudi Arabia: Women not allowed to drive cars or ride bicycles.

Egypt: Only males may confer citizenship; children born to women with foreign husbands are not conferred the benefits of citizenship.

igeria: Increasing undamentalist pressure the north; Shari'a ourts imposing severe entences, including ogging and death by toning, on women for exual impropriety.

waziland: Married women are legal minors, although those ho marry under civil law may e accorded the legal status of dults, if stipulated in a signed prenuptial agreement.

States Against Discrimination

Most of the world's governments are committed, on paper, to full equality for women. The Convention on the Elimination of All Forms of Discrimination Against Women (CEDAW), a UN treaty, was adopted in 1979 and came into force in 1981. It was the result of years of organizing by women, both within the United Nations and in dozens of countries around the world. The final impetus for drafting the treaty was the 1975 UN Women's Conference in Mexico.

CEDAW is not the first UN treaty concerning the status of women. Several earlier treaties on marriage rights, political rights, and trafficking set the stage for CEDAW, and remain important in their own right.

CEDAW establishes a universal set of standards and principles that are intended to serve as a template for shaping national policies towards the long-term goal of eliminating gender discrimination. Governments that ratify CEDAW are obliged to develop and implement policies and laws to eliminate discrimination against women within their country.

As with many international agreements, the practical effectiveness of CEDAW has been mixed. Many governments have ratified CEDAW without demonstrating much effort to comply with the treaty. Nonetheless, CEDAW establishes a platform of minimum expectations to which women's groups can – and do – hold governments accountable.

16

The UN Convention on the Elimination of All Forms of Discrimination Against Women (CEDAW)

status as of May 2002

169 countries – more than two-thirds of the members of the United Nations – are party to the Convention and an additional 3 have signed the treaty, but not ratified it.

states that have both signed and ratified the Convention

states that have signed but not ratified

states that have neither signed nor ratified

other countries

Polygyny
Percentage of married women,
aged 15 – 49, in polygynous unions
latest data since mid 1990s

50% and over — Benin, Guinea,
Burkina Faso

40% – 49% — Nigeria, Togo,
Mali, Senegal

30% – 39% — Uganda, Cameroon,
Côte d'Ivoire, Liberia,
Niger, Chad

20% – 29% — Malawi, Comoros,
Mozambique, Ghana,
Central African Rep,
Tanzania

10% – 19% — Burundi, Namibia,
Rwanda, Kenya,
Sudan, Zambia,
Zimbabwe

under 10% — Jordan, Morocco,
Nepal, Pakistan,
Yemen

4 | Households

The nature of families and of households is undergoing quite extraordinary changes. Both are smaller; more are headed by women, and more people live alone. Households are smallest in rich countries, having declined there to an average of 2.8 people per household. The number of one-person households is growing dramatically, the result of increases in unmarried adults and in elderly women living alone. Only in some northern African countries have household sizes increased.

More and more women around the world find themselves the only adult in the household. Of all lone-parent households, about 85 percent are headed by women. These are poorer than those headed by men. Households headed by elderly women living alone face the greatest economic disadvantages of all.

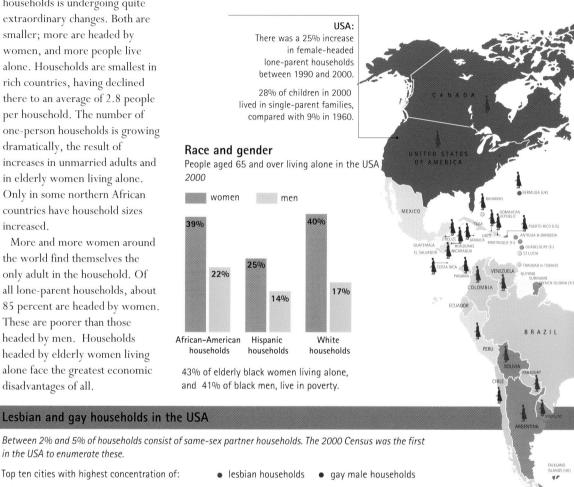

USA:
There was a 25% increase in female-headed lone-parent households between 1990 and 2000.

28% of children in 2000 lived in single-parent families, compared with 9% in 1960.

Race and gender
People aged 65 and over living alone in the USA 2000

women   men

African–American households: 39% women, 22% men
Hispanic households: 25% women, 14% men
White households: 40% women, 17% men

43% of elderly black women living alone, and 41% of black men, live in poverty.

Lesbian and gay households in the USA

Between 2% and 5% of households consist of same-sex partner households. The 2000 Census was the first in the USA to enumerate these.

Top ten cities with highest concentration of: ● lesbian households   ● gay male households

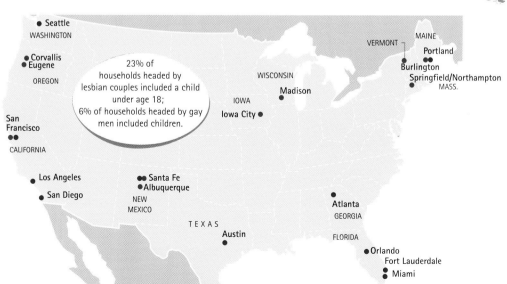

23% of households headed by lesbian couples included a child under age 18; 6% of households headed by gay men included children.

Seattle — WASHINGTON
Corvallis, Eugene — OREGON
San Francisco, Los Angeles, San Diego — CALIFORNIA
Santa Fe, Albuquerque — NEW MEXICO
Austin — TEXAS
WISCONSIN — Madison
IOWA — Iowa City
Atlanta — GEORGIA
Orlando, Fort Lauderdale, Miami — FLORIDA
VERMONT — Burlington
MAINE — Portland
Springfield/Northampton — MASS.

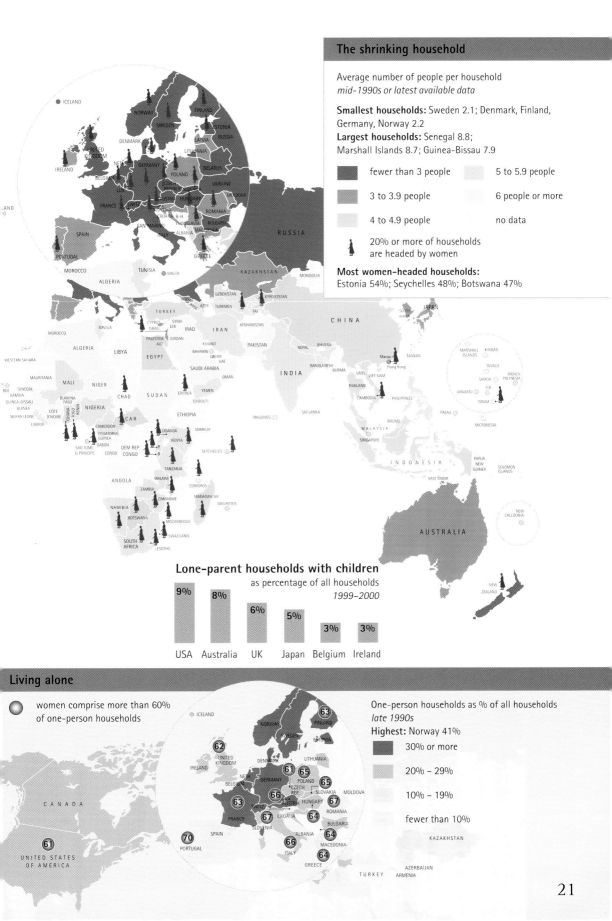

The shrinking household

Average number of people per household
mid-1990s or latest available data

Smallest households: Sweden 2.1; Denmark, Finland, Germany, Norway 2.2
Largest households: Senegal 8.8; Marshall Islands 8.7; Guinea-Bissau 7.9

- fewer than 3 people
- 3 to 3.9 people
- 4 to 4.9 people
- 5 to 5.9 people
- 6 people or more
- no data

20% or more of households are headed by women

Most women-headed households:
Estonia 54%; Seychelles 48%; Botswana 47%

Lone-parent households with children
as percentage of all households
1999–2000

USA	Australia	UK	Japan	Belgium	Ireland
9%	8%	6%	5%	3%	3%

Living alone

women comprise more than 60% of one-person households

One-person households as % of all households
late 1990s
Highest: Norway 41%

- 30% or more
- 20% – 29%
- 10% – 19%
- fewer than 10%

Map values: Finland 63; United Kingdom 62; France 63; Germany 61; Poland 65; Czech Rep. 65; Slovakia 65; Hungary 67; Austria 66; Switz 67; Croatia 64; Romania 64; Bulgaria 64; Albania 66; Macedonia 64; Italy 66; Greece 64; Portugal 70; United States of America 61

Marriage and Divorce

With the exception of the Caribbean region, which is notable for its relatively low rates of marriage, most women and men in the world spend most of their lives married. However, the nature of marriage varies widely from place to place, and between men and women.

Worldwide, women marry younger than men. In some places the gap is extreme. For example, in Niger, 70 percent of girls, but only 4 percent of boys are married by age 19; in Honduras, the figure is 30 percent of girls and 7 percent of boys.

The idea that married women "belong" to their husbands still dominates gender relations in most countries, and is often backed up by law. In some countries women need their husband's permission to buy or sell property, to have an abortion, to travel outside the country (see Map 2), or to take up employment. In some places, widows can even be "inherited" along with other possessions. The notion that women are the "property" of their husbands is a potent ideological prop of domestic violence (see Map 7).

Marriage is changing. Polygamy is being challenged in many of the countries where it is practiced. In most industrialized countries, the women are marrying later, and more women are not getting married, or cohabiting before marriage. Legal recognition for gay unions expands the boundaries of marriage (see Map 6).

Age of marriage

Average age of women at first marriage
1980, 1990, 1998
selected countries

	1980	1990	1998
Sweden	26	28	30
Denmark	25	28	30
Iceland	23	26	30
Norway	25	28	29
Finland	25	27	28
Ireland	24	28	28
Germany	23	26	28
Spain	24	25	27
UK	na	25	27
Canada	23	26	27
USA	23	25	26
Russia	23	23	23

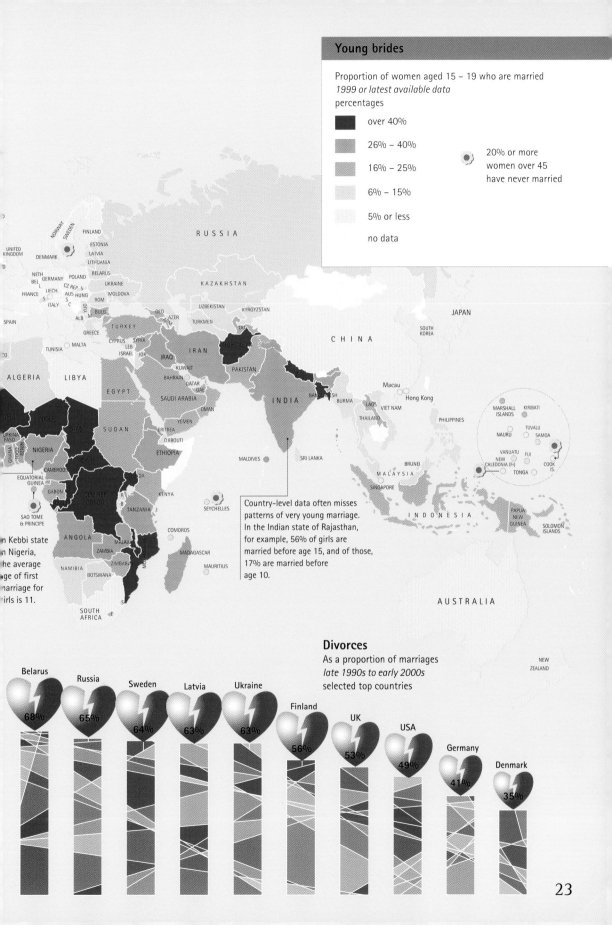

Proportion of women aged 15 – 19 who are married
1999 or latest available data
percentages

- over 40%
- 26% – 40%
- 16% – 25%
- 6% – 15%
- 5% or less
- no data

20% or more
women over 45
have never married

Country-level data often misses
patterns of very young marriage.
In the Indian state of Rajasthan,
for example, 56% of girls are
married before age 15, and of those,
17% are married before
age 10.

n Kebbi state
n Nigeria,
he average
ge of first
narriage for
irls is 11.

Divorces
As a proportion of marriages
late 1990s to early 2000s
selected top countries

- Belarus 68%
- Russia 65%
- Sweden 64%
- Latvia 63%
- Ukraine 63%
- Finland 56%
- UK 53%
- USA 49%
- Germany 41%
- Denmark 35%

23

Lesbians and gay men are increasingly visible in many countries. Lesbian and gay organizing over the past decade has been impressive. In some countries, governments are slowly responding to pressure to offer protection and recognition for lesbian and gay rights.

In other places, though, hatred of homosexuals is institutionalized and encouraged, and repression of lesbians and gay men remains severe. Lesbians are often raped, sometimes by family members, as a punishment or as a "treatment" for their homosexuality. While it is difficult to generalize about what provokes such strong homophobia, it is clear that the presence of lesbians and gay men challenges complacency about narrow definitions of what constitutes a family, a household, or "normal" sexual relationships. When women step outside of heterosexual norms, they are seen as being doubly subversive – both as members of a sexual minority, and also as women who are rejecting male authority.

World Health Organization 1991 removes homosexuality from its classification list of diseases.

Chile 1998 Criminalization of same-sex sexual relationships repealed.

Persecution and protection

high levels of violent attacks on lesbians, gays and transgendered people *since 1990 where known*

national legislation provides protection against discrimination *in most cases such protections apply to limited civil-society domains, such as job discrimination*

Safe havens

immigration laws allow the possibility of refugee asylum to gays and lesbians facing persecution in their home state

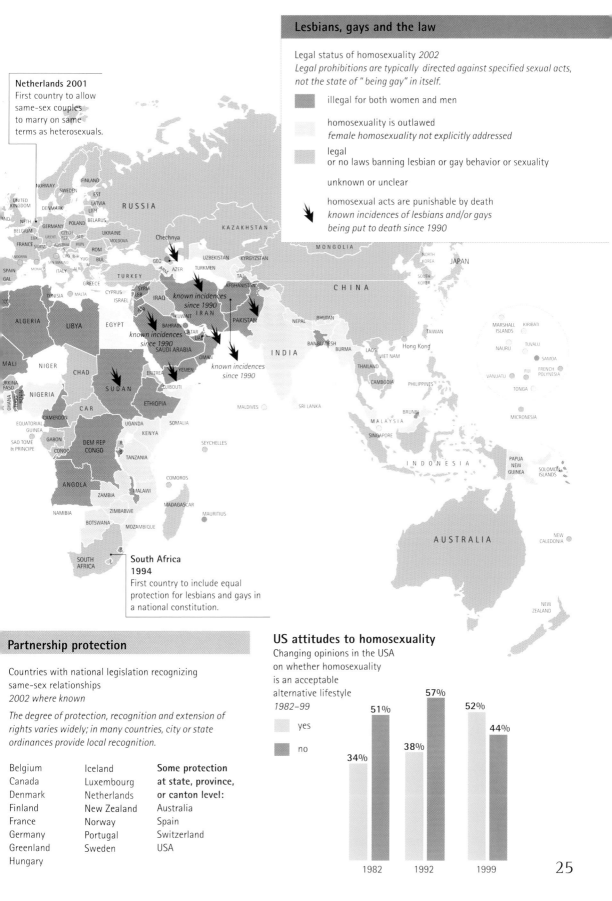

Lesbians, gays and the law

Legal status of homosexuality *2002*
Legal prohibitions are typically directed against specified sexual acts, not the state of " being gay" in itself.

- illegal for both women and men
- homosexuality is outlawed
  female homosexuality not explicitly addressed
- legal
  or no laws banning lesbian or gay behavior or sexuality
- unknown or unclear
- homosexual acts are punishable by death
  known incidences of lesbians and/or gays being put to death since 1990

Netherlands 2001
First country to allow same-sex couples to marry on same terms as heterosexuals.

South Africa 1994
First country to include equal protection for lesbians and gays in a national constitution.

known incidences since 1990

known incidences since 1990

known incidences since 1990

Partnership protection

Countries with national legislation recognizing same-sex relationships
2002 where known

The degree of protection, recognition and extension of rights varies widely; in many countries, city or state ordinances provide local recognition.

Belgium	Iceland	**Some protection**
Canada	Luxembourg	**at state, province,**
Denmark	Netherlands	**or canton level:**
Finland	New Zealand	Australia
France	Norway	Spain
Germany	Portugal	Switzerland
Greenland	Sweden	USA
Hungary		

US attitudes to homosexuality

Changing opinions in the USA on whether homosexuality is an acceptable alternative lifestyle
1982–99

- yes
- no

1982: 34% yes, 51% no
1992: 38% yes, 57% no
1999: 52% yes, 44% no

Domestic Violence

" Significant numbers of the world's population are routinely subject to torture, starvation, terrorism, humiliation, mutilation and even murder simply because they are female. Crimes such as these against any other group would be recognized as a civil and political emergency."

—Charlotte Bunch and Roxanna Carrillo

For millions of women, the home is the most dangerous place they could be. Far from being a place of safety, the family is often a cradle of violence. Women suffer cruelties in their homes every day, from all family members. Domestic violence is a means of keeping women "in their place," literally confined to relationship, household, or family structures defined by patriarchal authority. Violence against women sustains particular sexual, family, and household structures, and keeps women subordinate to them.

Domestic violence is the most ubiquitous constant in women's lives around the world. There is virtually no place where it is not a significant problem, and women of no race, class, or age are exempt from its reach. Statistics on domestic violence are notoriously unreliable. What information we do have about it is only available because of concerted campaigns by women to bring attention to this issue.

Violence against women is often ignored or even condoned by the state on the grounds that it is a "private" matter.

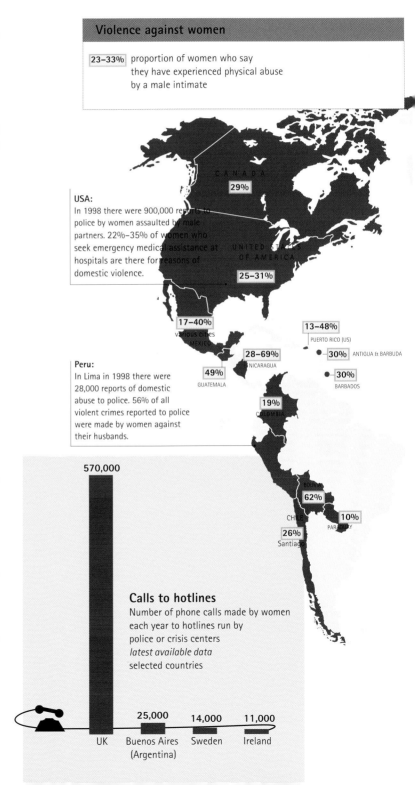

Violence against women

23–33% proportion of women who say they have experienced physical abuse by a male intimate

USA:
In 1998 there were 900,000 reports to police by women assaulted by male partners. 22%–35% of women who seek emergency medical assistance at hospitals are there for reasons of domestic violence.

Peru:
In Lima in 1998 there were 28,000 reports of domestic abuse to police. 56% of all violent crimes reported to police were made by women against their husbands.

CANADA **29%**

UNITED STATES OF AMERICA **25–31%**

17–40% various cities MEXICO

13–48% PUERTO RICO (US)

28–69% NICARAGUA

30% ANTIGUA & BARBUDA

49% GUATEMALA

30% BARBADOS

19% COLOMBIA

BOLIVIA **62%**

CHILE

26% Santiago

10% PARAGUAY

Calls to hotlines
Number of phone calls made by women each year to hotlines run by police or crisis centers
latest available data
selected countries

570,000

25,000

14,000

11,000

UK | Buenos Aires (Argentina) | Sweden | Ireland

Women's acceptance of domestic violence

Percentage of women who think it is acceptable for a husband to beat his wife for one or more specific reasons – burning food, arguing with him, going out without telling him, neglecting the children, refusing sex
1999–2001 selected countries

36% Malawi
77% Uganda
51% Zimbabwe
32% Armenia
52% Turkmenistan
29% Nepal
40% Haiti

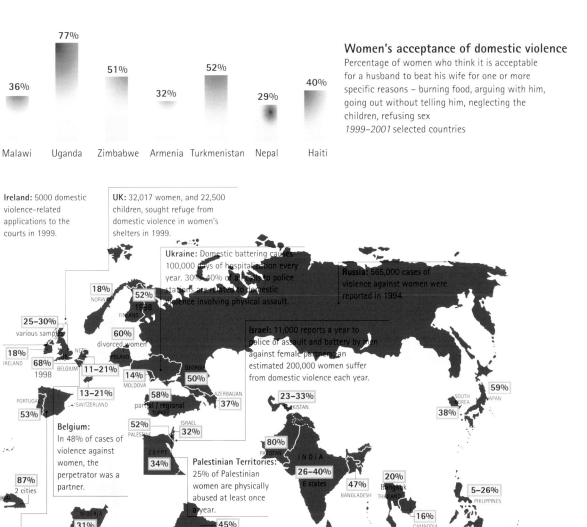

Ireland: 5000 domestic violence-related applications to the courts in 1999.

UK: 32,017 women, and 22,500 children, sought refuge from domestic violence in women's shelters in 1999.

Ukraine: Domestic battering causes 100,000 days of hospitalization every year. 30%–40% of all calls to police stations are related to domestic violence involving physical assault.

Russia: 565,000 cases of violence against women were reported in 1994.

Israel: 11,000 reports a year to police of assault and battery by men against female partners; an estimated 200,000 women suffer from domestic violence each year.

Belgium: In 48% of cases of violence against women, the perpetrator was a partner.

Palestinian Territories: 25% of Palestinian women are physically abused at least once a year.

Spain: In 2000 there were 22,000 cases of domestic violence against women reported to police.

Sri Lanka: 1,106 incidents of violence against women reported in the press in 1998, 26% of which were "domestic violence" reports.

18% NORWAY
52% 1998 FINLAND
25–30% various samples
18% IRELAND
60% divorced women
68% 1998 BELGIUM
11–21%
14% MOLDOVA
50% GEORGIA
58% partial / regional TURKEY
37% AZERBAIJAN
23–33% PAKISTAN
59% JAPAN
38% SOUTH KOREA
13–21% SWITZERLAND
53% PORTUGAL
52% PALESTINE
32% ISRAEL
80% PAKISTAN
87% 2 cities
31% NIGERIA
34% EGYPT
45% one district ETHIOPIA
41% two districts UGANDA
42% one district KENYA
60% TANZANIA
40% ZAMBIA
17–32% ZIMBABWE
13–29% SOUTH AFRICA
26–40% 6 states INDIA
47% BANGLADESH
20% Bangkok THAILAND
16% CAMBODIA
5–26% PHILIPPINES
12% INDONESIA
67% rural PAPUA NEW GUINEA
23–38% AUSTRALIA
20–35% NEW ZEALAND

Shelters for battered women
Year in which first shelter was opened

UK	Canada	Netherlands, USA, Australia	(West) Germany	Israel, Japan, South Africa, Sweden	Ireland	Denmark, Finland	India, Mexico	Thailand	Malaysia	Trinidad & Tobago	Greece	Philippines	Tunisia	Namibia	Russia	Mongolia	China
1971	1972	1974	1976	1977	1978	1979	1980	1981	1982	1987	1988	1989	1990	1993	1994	1995	1996

At least one woman in three in the world has been beaten, coerced into sex, or otherwise abused in her lifetime by a member of her family; for the majority of such women, the abuse is repeated over months or years. In an astonishing number of cases, "ordinary" domestic violence culminates in murder. Violence against women often escalates when the woman tries to leave an abusive relationship – this is when violent partners are most likely to turn to murder.

Some patterns of women-murder are culture and place-specific: dowry-burnings in India and Pakistan, bride-price murders in Zambia, gun-murders in the USA. "Honor killing" is a term used to identify a form of legally or socially sanctioned revenge exercised within a family against a woman who is deemed to have soiled the family's honor, usually through behavior that is judged to be sexually inappropriate. Women's human rights activists are increasing pressure on governments to take action against honor killings, but many governments are reluctant to do so.

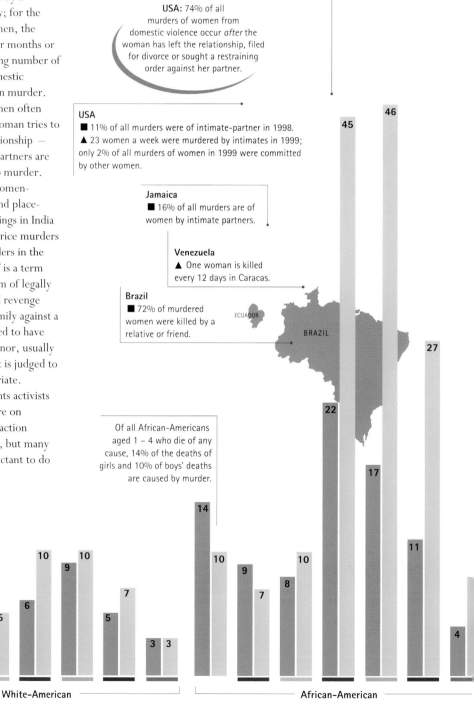

Canada
■ 15% of all homicides are of spouses.

USA: 74% of all murders of women from domestic violence occur *after* the woman has left the relationship, filed for divorce or sought a restraining order against her partner.

USA
■ 11% of all murders were of intimate-partner in 1998.
▲ 23 women a week were murdered by intimates in 1999; only 2% of all murders of women in 1999 were committed by other women.

Jamaica
■ 16% of all murders are of women by intimate partners.

Venezuela
▲ One woman is killed every 12 days in Caracas.

Brazil
■ 72% of murdered women were killed by a relative or friend.

ECUADOR

BRAZIL

Of all African-Americans aged 1 – 4 who die of any cause, 14% of the deaths of girls and 10% of boys' deaths are caused by murder.

46
45
27
22
17
14
11
10 10 10
9
8 9
7 7
6
5 5 5 5 5 5
4 4
3 3
<1

White-American   African-American

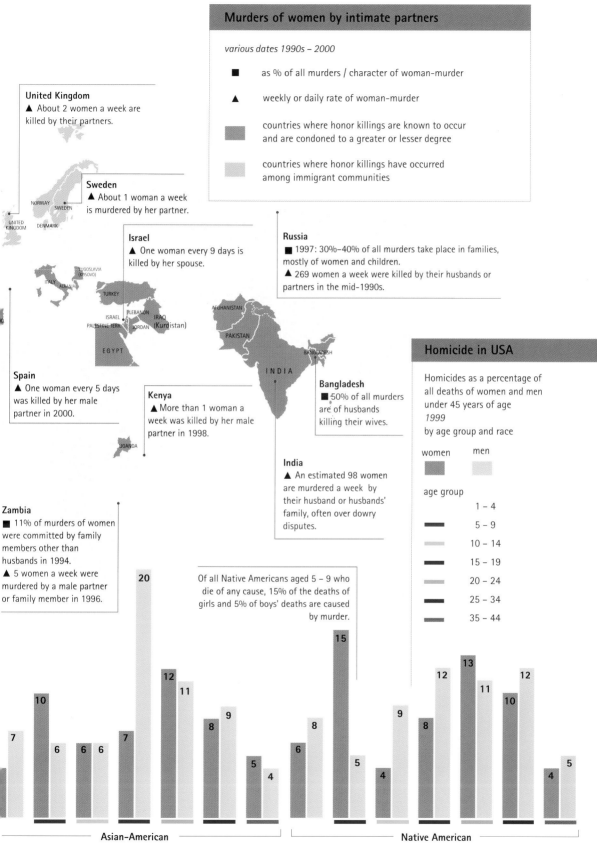

Murders of women by intimate partners

various dates 1990s – 2000

■ as % of all murders / character of woman-murder

▲ weekly or daily rate of woman-murder

countries where honor killings are known to occur and are condoned to a greater or lesser degree

countries where honor killings have occurred among immigrant communities

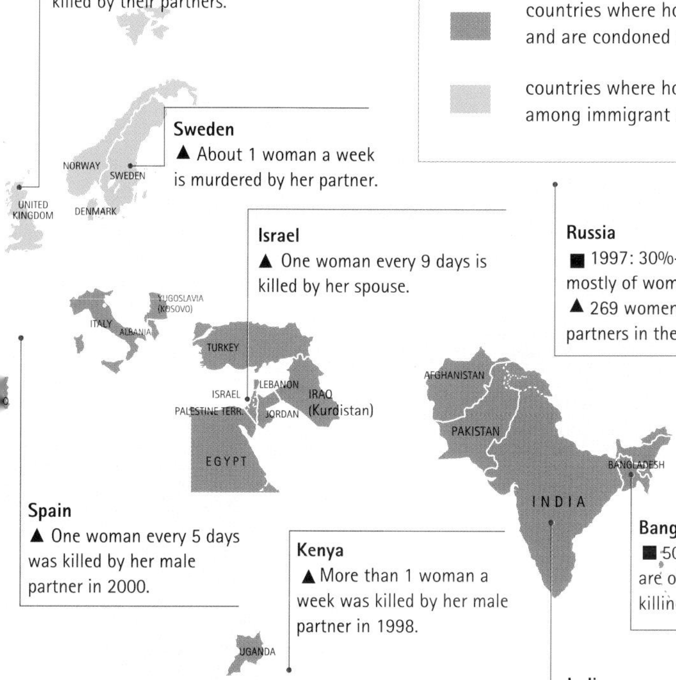

UNITED KINGDOM
NORWAY
SWEDEN
DENMARK
YUGOSLAVIA (KOSOVO)
ITALY
ALBANIA
TURKEY
LEBANON
ISRAEL
PALESTINE TERR.
JORDAN
IRAQ (Kurdistan)
EGYPT
AFGHANISTAN
PAKISTAN
INDIA
BANGLADESH
UGANDA

United Kingdom
▲ About 2 women a week are killed by their partners.

Sweden
▲ About 1 woman a week is murdered by her partner.

Israel
▲ One woman every 9 days is killed by her spouse.

Russia
■ 1997: 30%–40% of all murders take place in families, mostly of women and children.
▲ 269 women a week were killed by their husbands or partners in the mid-1990s.

Spain
▲ One woman every 5 days was killed by her male partner in 2000.

Kenya
▲ More than 1 woman a week was killed by her male partner in 1998.

Bangladesh
■ 50% of all murders are of husbands killing their wives.

India
▲ An estimated 98 women are murdered a week by their husband or husbands' family, often over dowry disputes.

Zambia
■ 11% of murders of women were committed by family members other than husbands in 1994.
▲ 5 women a week were murdered by a male partner or family member in 1996.

Homicide in USA

Homicides as a percentage of all deaths of women and men under 45 years of age
1999
by age group and race

women | men

age group
1 – 4
5 – 9
10 – 14
15 – 19
20 – 24
25 – 34
35 – 44

Of all Native Americans aged 5 – 9 who die of any cause, 15% of the deaths of girls and 5% of boys' deaths are caused by murder.

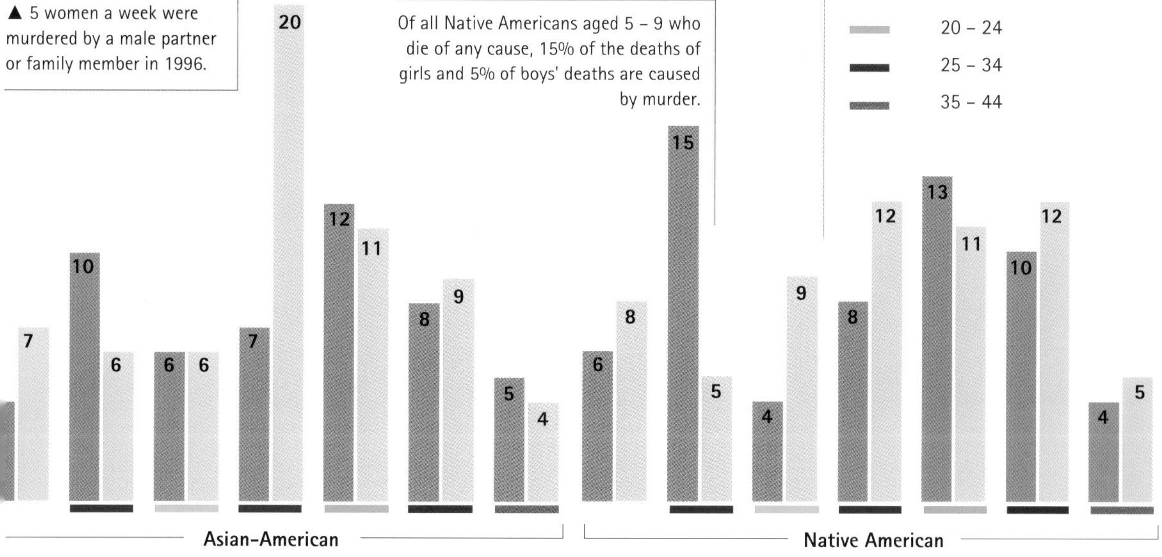

7
10
6
6
6
7
20
12
11
8
9
5
4
6
8
15
5
4
9
8
12
13
11
10
12
4
5
Asian-American
Native American

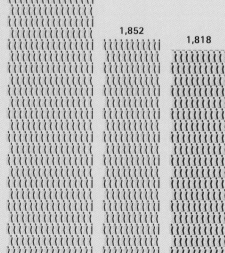

7,692

Deaths in pregnancy or childbirth
Number of women who die
per 100,000 pregnancies
2000

1,852

1,818

637

353

125

31

30

14

Sub-Saharan
Africa

South Asia

Middle East
and
North Africa

Latin America
and Caribbean

East Asia
and Pacific

Central
and
Eastern Europe,
CIS and Baltic States

Western
Europe

USA

Canada

9 | Motherhood

In many countries, women are engaged in childbearing for most of their adult lives. Nonetheless, on worldwide average, women are having fewer children than did their mothers and grandmothers. This trend reflects two main factors: the increasing availability of reproductive health services – including the liberalization of abortion laws (Map 11) – and incremental improvements in women's status and autonomy.

Sexual politics strongly influence the number of children women have or want to have. Almost everywhere, notions of what constitutes "normal" masculinity and femininity are defined in reference to fertility and family. It is common for both men's and women's social status to be pegged to the number of children they produce. Fertility rates are also shaped by marriage norms (Map 5), the prevalence of polygamy, son preference (Map 13), and presumptions about the sexual "needs" of men and women. Most surveys show that women typically want fewer children than do their male partners; thus, the gendered balance of power within the household is important in determining family size.

Government health, economic, and social security policies further shape family-size decisions; in much of the world, large families provide economic security and provide the primary social safety net. Additionally, national and international government population policies strongly influence fertility norms.

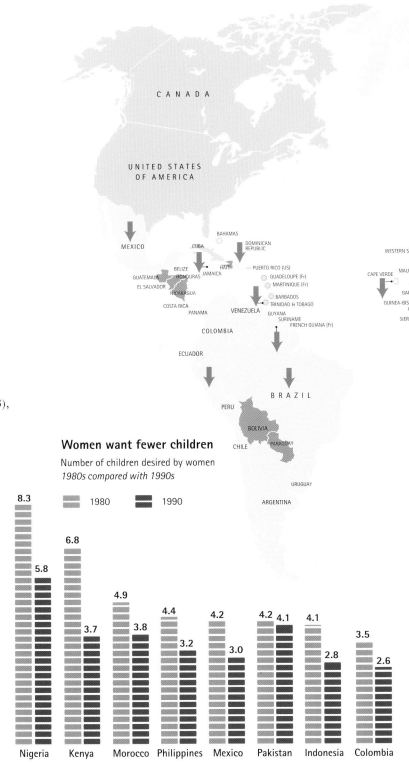

Women want fewer children

Number of children desired by women
1980s compared with 1990s

■ 1980   ■ 1990

Country	1980	1990
Nigeria	8.3	5.8
Kenya	6.8	3.7
Morocco	4.9	3.8
Philippines	4.4	3.2
Mexico	4.2	3.0
Pakistan	4.2	4.1
Indonesia	4.1	2.8
Colombia	3.5	2.6

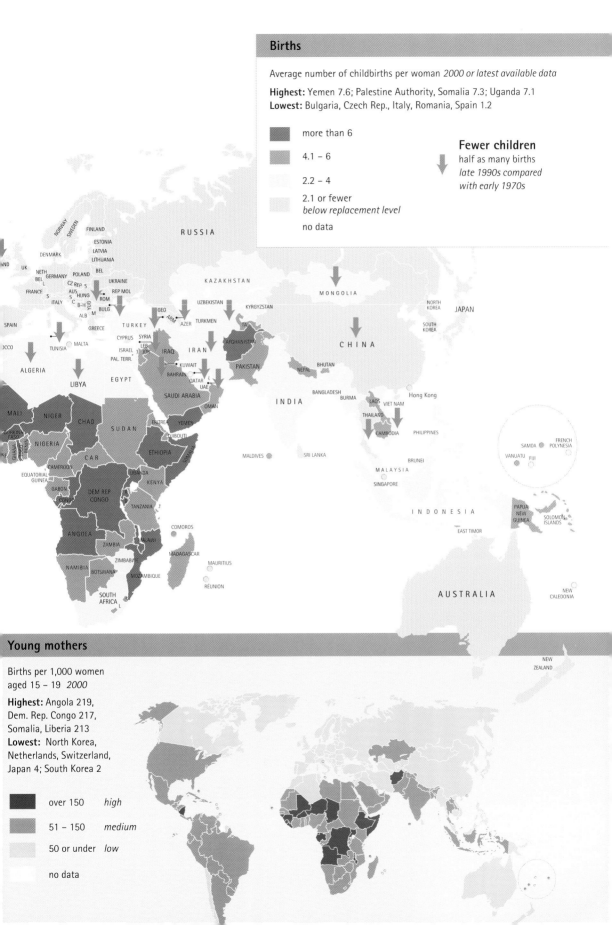

Births

Average number of childbirths per woman *2000 or latest available data*

Highest: Yemen 7.6; Palestine Authority, Somalia 7.3; Uganda 7.1
Lowest: Bulgaria, Czech Rep., Italy, Romania, Spain 1.2

- more than 6
- 4.1 – 6
- 2.2 – 4
- 2.1 or fewer
  below replacement level
- no data

Fewer children
half as many births
*late 1990s compared
with early 1970s*

Young mothers

Births per 1,000 women
aged 15 – 19 *2000*

Highest: Angola 219,
Dem. Rep. Congo 217,
Somalia, Liberia 213
Lowest: North Korea,
Netherlands, Switzerland,
Japan 4; South Korea 2

- over 150 *high*
- 51 – 150 *medium*
- 50 or under *low*
- no data

Since the 1970s, women's use of contraceptives has increased dramatically, and more than 50 percent of the world's women now use modern contraceptive methods. Access to reliable contraceptives is a powerful force in advancing women's liberation and autonomy.

Use of contraceptives remains uneven. Women in wealthy countries and urban areas generally have the best access to contraceptive services. Female sterilization remains the most common contraceptive method.

The politics of contraceptives development and distribution are complex and troubling. Abuses are common. In the past few decades, governments of several countries, including China, India, and the USA, have imposed programs of forced sterilization on minority or poor women. Global pharmaceutical companies have aggressively marketed unsafe or experimental contraceptives to poor women. Women still face the dilemma that the safest contraceptives are not the most effective, while the most effective are not necessarily the safest.

Emergency contraception

■ dedicated emergency contraceptive drugs are available
2001

"Emergency contraception" (EC) prevents pregnancy after intercourse has occurred. EC methods include special doses of birth control pills or insertion of an IUD. EC can be used up to three days after intercourse, and offers protection for women who have been raped, experienced contraceptive failure, or engaged in unprotected sex. RU486 (Mifepristone) is a drug that produces a miscarriage in the first weeks of pregnancy. Because it is a non-surgical abortifacient, RU 486 has been particularly controversial.

Mifepristone approved for use
2002

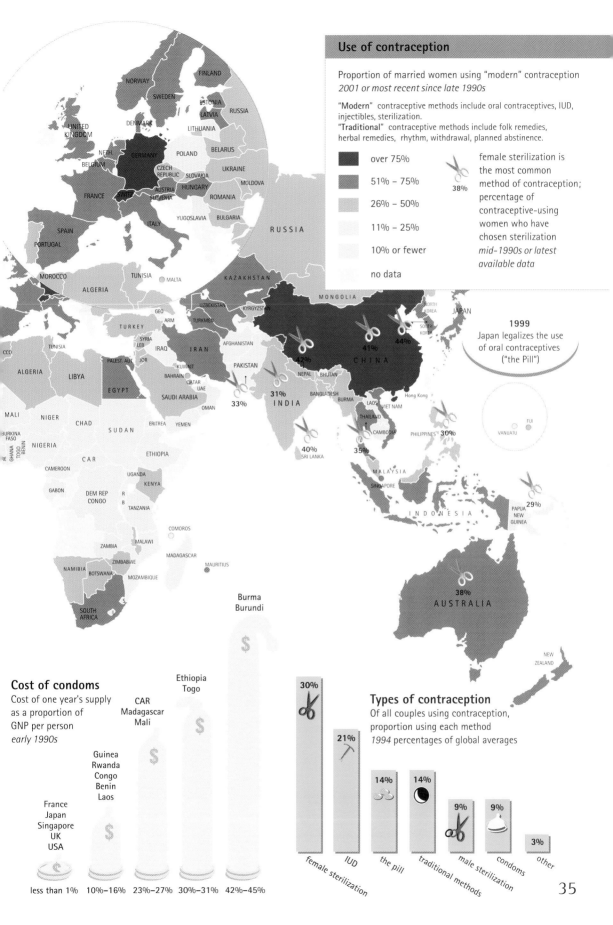

Use of contraception

Proportion of married women using "modern" contraception
2001 or most recent since late 1990s

"**Modern**" contraceptive methods include oral contraceptives, IUD, injectibles, sterilization.
"**Traditional**" contraceptive methods include folk remedies, herbal remedies, rhythm, withdrawal, planned abstinence.

- over 75%
- 51% – 75%
- 26% – 50%
- 11% – 25%
- 10% or fewer
- no data

female sterilization is the most common method of contraception; percentage of contraceptive-using women who have chosen sterilization *mid-1990s or latest available data*

1999
Japan legalizes the use of oral contraceptives ("the Pill")

Cost of condoms

Cost of one year's supply as a proportion of GNP per person *early 1990s*

France Japan Singapore UK USA	Guinea Rwanda Congo Benin Laos	CAR Madagascar Mali	Ethiopia Togo	Burma Burundi
less than 1%	10%–16%	23%–27%	30%–31%	42%–45%

Types of contraception

Of all couples using contraception, proportion using each method *1994 percentages of global averages*

- female sterilization 30%
- IUD 21%
- the pill 14%
- traditional methods 14%
- male sterilization 9%
- condoms 9%
- other 3%

35

There are an estimated 25 million to 30 million legal abortions in the world each year, and another 20 million unsafe, illegal abortions. Most women in the world who seek abortions are married, or live in stable unions, and already have children.

The struggle over abortion rights is at its heart a struggle about women's autonomy. The extent to which women control their reproductive choices affects their freedom in all other spheres: their participation in the economy, education, the household, and in political and civic arenas, as well as their degree of economic and social autonomy from men.

The legal status of abortion does not fully reflect the reality of abortion availability. In countries where abortions are legal, it does not necessarily mean they are available. Myriad factors affect women's actual access to abortion services, including their class, race, age, and geographic location. In some countries where abortion is legal, government support for it is nonetheless weak, and governments can and do undercut the availability of abortion services.

Still, the legal context of abortion is critically important. Restrictive legislation compels women to choose between unsafe abortions or unwanted births. Millions of women each year are desperate enough to seek clandestine abortions; tens of thousands die as a result. Even the most restrictive abortion laws typically allow some exceptions – for example, when pregnancy

threatens the woman's life – but a surprising number of governments do not allow abortions even when the pregnancy is the result of rape or incest.

Since the 1980s, the worldwide trend has been towards more liberal abortion laws – almost entirely due to persistent feminist activism. Nonetheless, about one-quarter of the world's women still live in countries with highly restrictive abortion laws.

In 2002, 86% of all US counties were not served by an abortion provider

Anti-abortion backlash
USA and Canada *1992–2002*
• 7 abortion clinic workers murdered
• 15 attempted murders
• 97 arsons and bombings of clinics
• 272 additional death threats
• 443 stalking incidents against workers or patients
• 654 anthrax mail threats received

Deaths from illegal abortions
Percentage of total deaths, by region *2001*

Each year, at least 20 million unsafe abortions take place, and 80,000 women die from the complications that follow.

Europe <1%
Latin America 6%
North America <1%
Africa 44%
Asia 49%

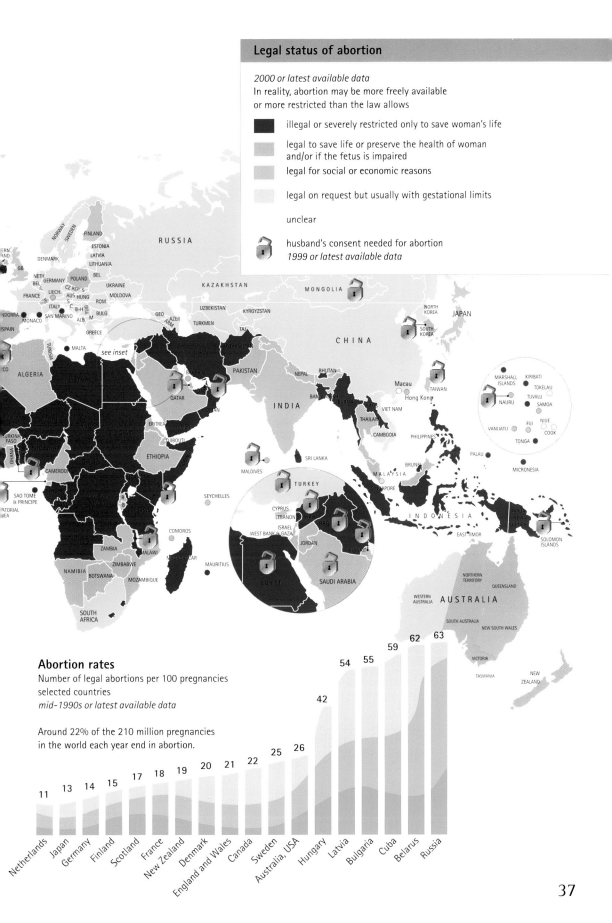

Legal status of abortion

2000 or latest available data
In reality, abortion may be more freely available
or more restricted than the law allows

- illegal or severely restricted only to save woman's life
- legal to save life or preserve the health of woman and/or if the fetus is impaired
- legal for social or economic reasons
- legal on request but usually with gestational limits
- unclear
- husband's consent needed for abortion *1999 or latest available data*

Abortion rates

Number of legal abortions per 100 pregnancies
selected countries
mid-1990s or latest available data

Around 22% of the 210 million pregnancies
in the world each year end in abortion.

Country	Rate
Netherlands	11
Japan	13
Germany	14
Finland	15
Scotland	17
France	18
New Zealand	19
Denmark	20
England and Wales	21
Canada	22
Sweden	25
Australia, USA	26
Hungary	42
Latvia	54
Bulgaria	55
Cuba	59
Belarus	62
Russia	63

37

Maternal Mortality

Each year, about 200 million women become pregnant; for over half a million of them, this will kill them. Another 50 million women will suffer long-term disability or illness as a consequence of pregnancy and childbirth. Of all the health measures monitored by the World Health Organization, the largest discrepancy between rich and poor countries occurs in maternal mortality. Most of these deaths could be prevented: by providing basic prenatal health care, improving maternal nutrition, and by providing the legal, social, and health support that would allow women to avoid unwanted pregnancies.

A recent UNICEF report described the global epidemic of maternal mortality this way: "How can such a heavy burden of death, disease, and disability have continued for so long with so little outcry? In part, the conspiracy of silence surrounding this issue is a reflection of the fact that women are conditioned not to complain, but to cope… As one midwife has put it: 'If hundreds of thousands of men were suffering and dying every year, alone and in fear and in agony, or if millions upon millions of men were being injured and disabled and humiliated, sustaining massive and untreated injuries and wounds to their genitalia, leaving them in constant pain, infertile, and incontinent and in dread of having sex, then we would all have heard about this issue long ago and something would have been done'."

Race in USA
maternal mortality, late 1990s, deaths per 100,000 live births: white women 5; Hispanic women 10; Asian/ Pacific Islanders 11; Native Americans 12; African American women 20.

Medical causes of maternal mortality
1990s
percentage distribution of maternal deaths

other direct causes (eg ectopic pregnancy) 8%
other indirect causes (eg anemia) 19%
obstructed labor 8%
hypertensive disorders 12%
severe bleeding 25%
unsafe abortions 13%
infections 15%

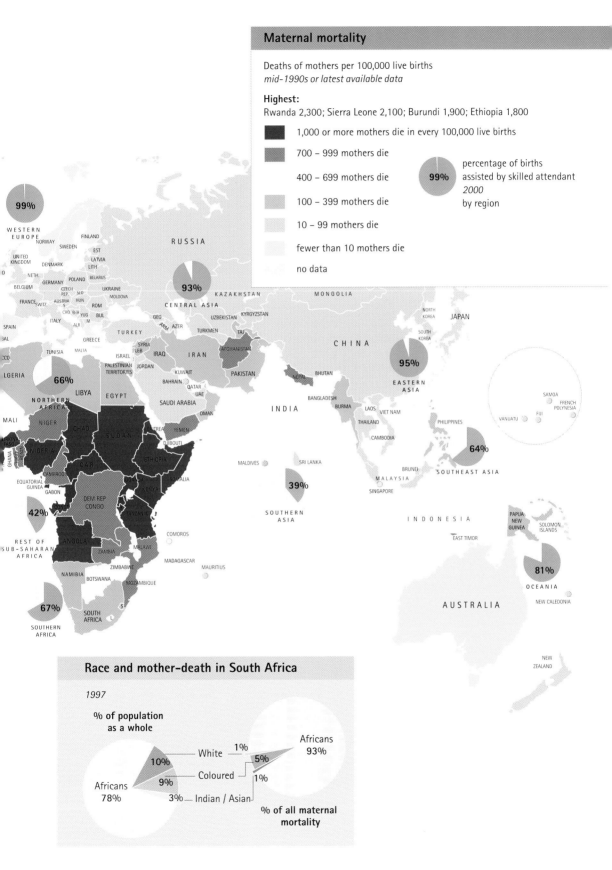

Maternal mortality

Deaths of mothers per 100,000 live births
mid-1990s or latest available data

Highest:
Rwanda 2,300; Sierra Leone 2,100; Burundi 1,900; Ethiopia 1,800

1,000 or more mothers die in every 100,000 live births

700 – 999 mothers die

400 – 699 mothers die

100 – 399 mothers die

10 – 99 mothers die

fewer than 10 mothers die

no data

99% percentage of births assisted by skilled attendant *2000* by region

WESTERN EUROPE **99%**

NORWAY SWEDEN FINLAND EST LATVIA LITH

UNITED KINGDOM DENMARK NETH. GERMANY POLAND BELARUS

BELGIUM CZECH REP. UKRAINE MOLDOVA

FRANCE SWITZ. AUSTRIA HUN ROM BUL

SPAIN ITALY CRO B-H YUG M ALB GREECE

SLO SLA

PORTUGAL

RUSSIA

CENTRAL ASIA **93%**

KAZAKHSTAN MONGOLIA

GEO ARM AZER UZBEKISTAN KYRGYZSTAN TURKMEN TAJ

TUNISIA MALTA TURKEY SYRIA LEB IRAQ IRAN AFGHANISTAN

ISRAEL PALESTINIAN TERRITORIES JORDAN KUWAIT PAKISTAN

MOROCCO

ALGERIA **66%** LIBYA EGYPT BAHRAIN QATAR UAE

NORTHERN AFRICA SAUDI ARABIA OMAN

MALI NIGER CHAD SUDAN ERITREA YEMEN

BURKINA FASO NIGERIA DJIBOUTI

GHANA CAMEROON C.A.R. ETHIOPIA

EQUATORIAL GUINEA GABON UGANDA SOMALIA KENYA

42% DEM REP CONGO TANZANIA

REST OF SUB-SAHARAN AFRICA ANGOLA ZAMBIA MALAWI COMOROS

NAMIBIA BOTSWANA ZIMBABWE MOZAMBIQUE MADAGASCAR MAURITIUS

67% SOUTH AFRICA

SOUTHERN AFRICA

NORTH KOREA JAPAN

CHINA SOUTH KOREA

NEPAL BHUTAN EASTERN ASIA **95%**

BANGLADESH BURMA LAOS

INDIA THAILAND VIET NAM

CAMBODIA PHILIPPINES

MALDIVES SRI LANKA

39% BRUNEI MALAYSIA SINGAPORE

SOUTHERN ASIA

SOUTHEAST ASIA **64%**

INDONESIA EAST TIMOR

PAPUA NEW GUINEA SOLOMON ISLANDS

SAMOA FRENCH POLYNESIA

VANUATU FIJI

81% OCEANIA NEW CALEDONIA

AUSTRALIA

NEW ZEALAND

Race and mother-death in South Africa

1997

% of population as a whole

Africans 78%

White 10%

Coloured 9%

Indian / Asian 3%

% of all maternal mortality

Africans 93%

White 1%

Coloured 5%

Indian / Asian 1%

Son Preference

Everywhere, boys tend to be privileged over girls. A cultural preference for sons over daughters is almost universal. But in a few places, this preference is acted out in ways that produce demographic distortion.

Sex ratios provide the surest evidence of extreme son preference. The biological norm is for about 95 girls to be born for every 100 boys, but boy infants have a naturally higher mortality rate so by early childhood the numbers should be roughly equal. In several countries, however, including South Korea, India, China, Bangladesh and Pakistan, the sex ratio is so severely skewed, with as few as 80 girls per 100 boys, that it is now causing widespread social distortions. Among other consequences, a shortage of women seems to be contributing to local and regional increases in trafficking and kidnapping of women (see also Map 20).

Son preference takes several forms, sometimes starting in the womb. In some places prenatal tests are used to detect female fetuses, which are then aborted. Such testing is prohibited in China, South Korea, and India, but these laws are weakly enforced. Female infanticide is common in some places, with girl infants killed within hours or days of birth. The neglect of girls – such as feeding them less or withholding medical attention – is chronic in many regions. Son preference reflects the combined forces of economics, culture and religion. As smaller families become the norm, evidence suggests that the pressure to have sons accelerates. Girls are widely considered to have a lower economic value than boys – a view often strengthened by marriage, dowry and inheritance practices. Son preference used to be thought of as a practice of the poor, but evidence suggests the opposite – increasing affluence magnifies perceptions of the greater worth of boys.

Choosing sons

Number of girls born per 100 boys by birth order

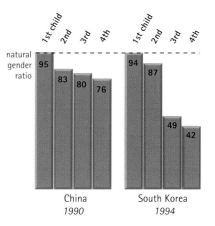

China 1990

South Korea 1994

Endangering daughters

Trends in birth sex ratios: Number of girls per 100 boys

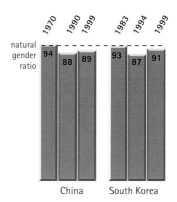

China   South Korea

Missing girls

The gap between the number of girls and women in the population and the number that would be expected if there were no discrimination.

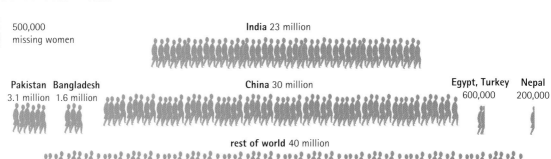

500,000 missing women

India 23 million

Pakistan 3.1 million   Bangladesh 1.6 million   China 30 million   Egypt, Turkey 600,000   Nepal 200,000

rest of world 40 million

Unnatural selection

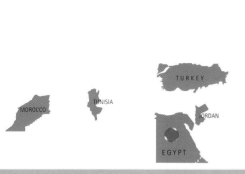

▮ strong demographic evidence of son preference *2000*

▮ other countries

◌ widespread use of prenatal sex selection techniques and selective abortions of female fetuses

● infant mortality rate higher for girls than boys

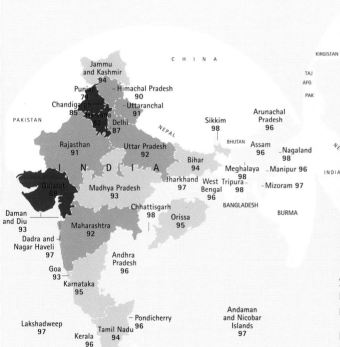

Sex ratios of children in India
Number of 0- to 6-year-old girls
per 100 boys *2001*

Natural gender ratio
of 0- to 6-year-olds:
105 girls per 100 boys

India 1991: 94.5 girls per 100 boys
India 2001: 92.7 girls per 100 boys

Sex ratios at birth in China
Number of girls born
per 100 boys *1999*

Natural gender ratio at birth: 95 girls per 100 boys
China 1990: 88 girls per 100 boys
China 1999: 89.4 girls per 100 boys

Evidence of son preference varies widely across India and China. The Punjab–Haryana–Himachal Pradesh belt in northwest India is sometimes dubbed "India's Bermuda Triangle" – where girls vanish without a trace. In 1991 two states and territories in India had ratios below 88 girls per 100 boys; in 2001 there were five. In China, son preference appears strongest in urban areas, where small-family policies are most vigorously enforced.

14 | Population Policies

Governments are key players in the reproductive lives of women. To the extent that governments, or private donors and agencies, provide access to reproductive health support services, their involvement in population issues is essential and beneficial.

But when control of women's fertility becomes construed as a matter of national or international policy, there is cause for concern. Over several decades, the reproductive behavior of poor women and those in developing countries has been defined as especially "problematic." Around the world, many governments have adopted coercive population policies – some encouraging and others discouraging growth. Such policies, typically enacted with external financial and political encouragement, have taken a heavy toll on women's rights and health.

CANADA

UNITED STATES OF AMERICA

MEXICO

BAHAMAS

CUBA
JAMAICA
BELIZE
GUATEMALA   HONDURAS
EL SALVADOR
NICARAGUA
COSTA RICA
PANAMA

HAITI   DOMINICAN REPUBLIC
ST KITTS &   ANTIGUA & BARBUDA
NEVIS   DOMINICA
ST LUCIA
ST VINCENT & GRENAD.   BARBADOS
GRENADA   TRINIDAD & TOBAGO
VENEZUELA   GUYANA
SURINAME

CAPE VERDE
MAUR
GAM
GUINEA
SIER

COLOMBIA

ECUADOR

PERU

BRAZIL

BOLIVIA

CHILE   PARAGUAY

ARGENTINA   URUGUAY

International population assistance

Donors and recipients of overseas population programs *2001*

major donors for overseas population programs *gave more than US$10 million*

main recipients of external population assistance *received more than US$10 million each*

View from the top

Governments' views on fertility rates in their own country
2001

- too high
- too low
- satisfactory
- no data

Funding bodies

Sources for international population assistance *1999*

direct assistance from developed countries **63%**

World Bank loans **20%**

Private foundations and NGOs **11%**

Biggest donors among private foundations/NGOs:
Bill & Melinda Gates Foundation (USA)
Marie Stopes International (UK)
Ford Foundation (USA)
Packard Foundation (USA)
Population Council (USA)
MacArthur Foundation (USA)
Rockefeller Foundation (USA)
Wellcome Trust (UK)

Changing views

1974–2001
Governments' views on fertility rates in their own country
2001

- too high
- too low

25% 14% 17%   28% 43% 45%
1974 1991 2001 1974 1991 2001

43

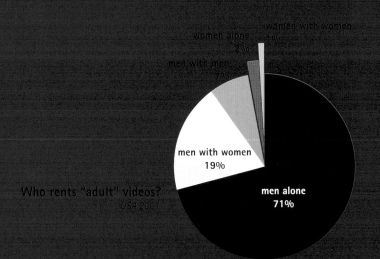

women with women
1%

women alone
2%

men with men
7%

men with women
19%

men alone
71%

Who rents "adult" videos?
USA 2001

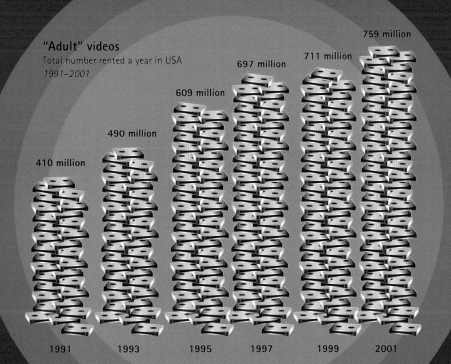

"Adult" videos
Total number rented a year in USA
1991–2001

410 million

490 million

609 million

697 million

711 million

759 million

1991   1993   1995   1997   1999   2001

15 Breast Cancer

Breast cancer is the most common cancer among women. Worldwide over 1 million new cases are diagnosed each year. The incidence of breast cancer is highest in industrialized countries. Europe and North America, home to under one fifth of the world's women, account for half of the world's breast cancer cases. The lowest rates of breast cancer are found in Asia.

One in eight women in industrialized countries will develop breast cancer over an 85-year lifespan. Thirty years ago, this number was 1 in 20. Worldwide, breast cancer rates have increased 26 percent since 1980. Breast cancer activists are increasingly certain that environmental factors, including exposure to plastics-based estrogen-mimicking chemicals, are responsible for the near-epidemic rates of the disease.

In most of Western Europe and North America, the proportion of women who die from breast cancer has been steadily dropping since the late 1980s, a trend attributed to earlier diagnosis and better treatment. However, the benefits of advanced medical care are not evenly distributed. For example, in the USA, the diagnosed incidence of breast cancer is higher among white women than Black, but Black women are more likely to die from it. This difference is largely a function of unequal access to medical care.

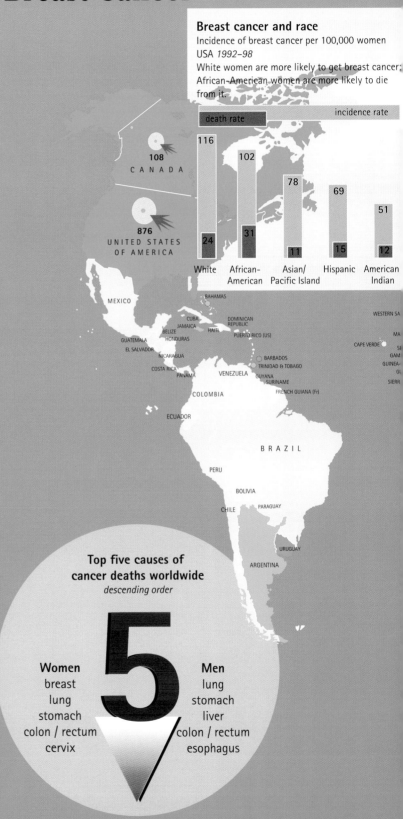

Breast cancer and race
Incidence of breast cancer per 100,000 women
USA *1992–98*
White women are more likely to get breast cancer; African-American women are more likely to die from it.

death rate   incidence rate

	White	African-American	Asian/Pacific Island	Hispanic	American Indian
incidence	116	102	78	69	51
death	24	31	11	15	12

108
CANADA

876
UNITED STATES OF AMERICA

MEXICO
BAHAMAS
CUBA
JAMAICA
BELIZE
HONDURAS
GUATEMALA
EL SALVADOR
HAITI
DOMINICAN REPUBLIC
PUERTO RICO (US)
NICARAGUA
COSTA RICA
PANAMA
BARBADOS
TRINIDAD & TOBAGO
VENEZUELA
GUYANA
SURINAME
FRENCH GUIANA (Fr)
COLOMBIA
ECUADOR
PERU
BRAZIL
BOLIVIA
CHILE
PARAGUAY
URUGUAY
ARGENTINA

WESTERN SA
MA
CAPE VERDE
GAM
GUINEA-
GU
SIERR

Top five causes of cancer deaths worldwide
descending order

5

Women
breast
lung
stomach
colon / rectum
cervix

Men
lung
stomach
liver
colon / rectum
esophagus

ICELAND

NORWAY
FINLAND
SWEDEN
ESTONIA
LATVIA RUSSIA
LITHUANIA

277
UNITED
KINGDOM
27 DENMARK
GERMANY

IRELAND
NETH.
POLAND
BELARUS
BELGIUM
LUX. **368**
CZECH
REPUBLIC SLOVAKIA
UKRAINE
MOLDOVA
SWITZ.
AUSTRIA HUNGARY
222
FRANCE
SLOVENIA ROMANIA
CROATIA B-H
ITALY YUGOSLAVIA BULGARIA
ALBANIA MACEDONIA

SPAIN
PORTUGAL
GREECE
229

MOROCCO TUNISIA MALTA
ALGERIA KAZAKHSTAN

382
RUSSIA

Breast cancer

Incidence per 100,000 women *2000*
world age standardized rate

75 or over

50 – 74

25 – 49

under 25

no data

The weekly death toll

number of women
who died each week
from breast cancer
in 2000

MONGOLIA

UZBEKISTAN KYRGYZSTAN
GEO AZER
TURKEY ARM TURKMEN
TAJ
53
CYPRUS SYRIA
ISRAEL LEB IRAQ IRAN AFGHANISTAN
JOR
KUWAIT PAKISTAN NEPAL BHUTAN
BAHRAIN QATAR
UAE
SAUDI ARABIA **781**
INDIA BANGLADESH BURMA
OMAN

NORTH
KOREA
JAPAN
SOUTH
KOREA
160

554 C H I N A

TAIWAN

Hong Kong

TUNISIA
ALGERIA LIBYA
EGYPT
MALI
NIGER CHAD SUDAN ERITREA YEMEN
DJIBOUTI
NIGERIA
KINA
SO
GUINEA TOGO BENIN
CAR ETHIOPIA
CAMEROON
EQUATORIAL
GUINEA
GABON
CONGO DEM REP
CONGO R
B UGANDA SOMALIA
KENYA
TANZANIA

LAOS VIET NAM
THAILAND
CAMBODIA PHILIPPINES

SAMOA
VANUATU FIJI

SRI LANKA

BRUNEI
M A L A Y S I A
SINGAPORE

ANGOLA
ZAMBIA
NAMIBIA ZIMBABWE
BOTSWANA MOZAMBIQUE
COMOROS
MALAWI
MADAGASCAR
MAURITIUS
S
SOUTH
AFRICA L

I N D O N E S I A

PAPUA
NEW
GUINEA
EAST TIMOR
SOLOMON
ISLANDS

52
A U S T R A L I A

NEW
ZEALAND

Highest death rate

◄Number of women who die from breast cancer per 100,000 women
2000

◄3	50	48	47	46	45	42	41	40	39	38	36	35	34	33	32	31

| mark | Iceland | Belgium, UK | Neths | Germany, Hungary | Switzerland | Austria | Luxembourg | Italy | Uruguay | Czech Rep, France | Canada, Croatia, New Zealand, Norway | Ireland, Slovenia | Barbados, Sweden | Israel | Spain, USA | Estonia, Finland, Greece, Portugal |

Over 40 million people in the world are HIV infected. Seventy percent of them live in Sub-Saharan Africa. More than half are women. Without access to the medical advances available in richer countries, most will die.

Women's social and sexual status puts them at particular risk of infection. Sexual relations between men and women are often framed by violence, coercion, and the presumption of men's "right" of sexual access to women. Many women are not able to negotiate safe sexual behavior with male partners. Higher illiteracy rates for women, and certain social arrangements such as polygamy add to their burden of risk.

Women, the traditional caretakers of families, often have no one to care for them when they are ill. The deaths of women leave whole households without support. Worldwide, a huge population of AIDS orphans, totaling an estimated 14 million children, has been left in the wake of the disease – 11 million of them in sub-Saharan Africa. Girls who are orphaned are particularly vulnerable to sexual and economic exploitation and thus, in turn, to HIV infection.

Men are increasingly seeking young girls as sexual partners, presuming them to be safe from infection. This is both a local and global pattern: international trafficking in women (Map 20) increasingly involves ever-younger girls. Women are becoming infected on average at an age five to ten years younger than men.

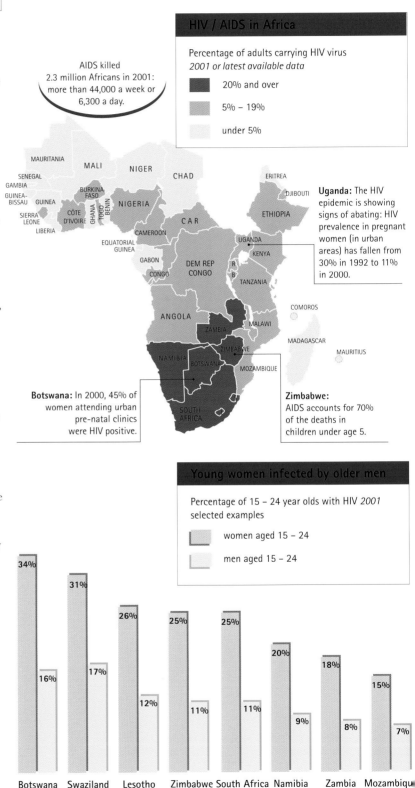

HIV / AIDS in Africa

Percentage of adults carrying HIV virus
2001 or latest available data

- 20% and over
- 5% – 19%
- under 5%

AIDS killed 2.3 million Africans in 2001: more than 44,000 a week or 6,300 a day.

Uganda: The HIV epidemic is showing signs of abating: HIV prevalence in pregnant women (in urban areas) has fallen from 30% in 1992 to 11% in 2000.

Botswana: In 2000, 45% of women attending urban pre-natal clinics were HIV positive.

Zimbabwe: AIDS accounts for 70% of the deaths in children under age 5.

Young women infected by older men

Percentage of 15 – 24 year olds with HIV *2001* selected examples

- women aged 15 – 24
- men aged 15 – 24

Country	women 15–24	men 15–24
Botswana	34%	16%
Swaziland	31%	17%
Lesotho	26%	12%
Zimbabwe	25%	11%
South Africa	25%	11%
Namibia	20%	9%
Zambia	18%	8%
Mozambique	15%	7%

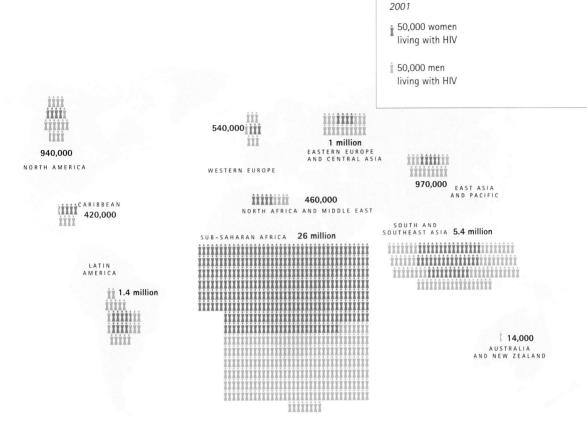

940,000
NORTH AMERICA

540,000

1 million
EASTERN EUROPE
AND CENTRAL ASIA

WESTERN EUROPE

970,000 EAST ASIA
AND PACIFIC

CARIBBEAN
420,000

460,000
NORTH AFRICA AND MIDDLE EAST

SOUTH AND
SOUTHEAST ASIA **5.4 million**

SUB-SAHARAN AFRICA **26 million**

LATIN
AMERICA

1.4 million

14,000
AUSTRALIA
AND NEW ZEALAND

The weekly death toll

Number of people who died each week
from HIV / AIDS in 2001
selected examples

South Africa	6,923
Zimbabwe	3,846
Thailand	1,058
Haiti	577
Botswana	500
USA	288
Cambodia	231
Ukraine	212
France	15
Germany	13
UK	9

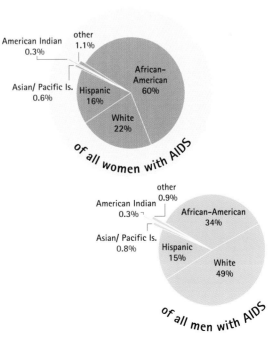

Race ethnicity and gender
AIDS cases in the USA *1985–2000*

other
1.1%
American Indian
0.3%

Asian/ Pacific Is.
0.6%

Hispanic
16%

African-
American
60%

White
22%

of all women with AIDS

other
0.9%
American Indian
0.3%

Asian/ Pacific Is.
0.8%

Hispanic
15%

African-American
34%

White
49%

of all men with AIDS

49

Notions of "appropriate" masculinity and femininity are deeply embedded within, and structured by, participation in sports and athletics. Men who do not show much interest in sports are often considered to be suspiciously un-manly; women who want to develop body strength and athletic skills still have an uphill struggle against conventional definitions of femininity. Athletic women and girls are often stigmatized and socially "policed" by being labeled as lesbians. In many countries, these conventional barriers and attitudes are changing – but only after decades of challenges by women sports pioneers, persistence by women who have long dealt with being "gender outcasts," and after prolonged legal battles.

The participation of women in the Olympics mirrors the larger struggle over women in sports. A gender gap remains in the money and media attention showered on men's and women's sports – even in sports where women have achieved prominence. At the Wimbledon Lawn Tennis Championship in 2002, for example, the winner of the men's singles received £525,000, while the women's singles champion received only £486,000.

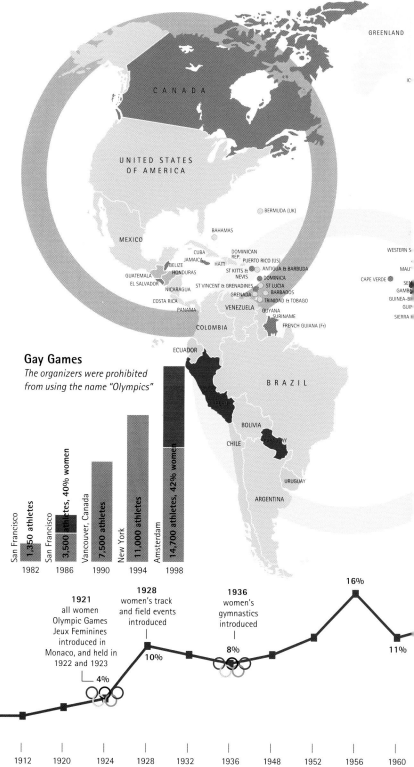

Gay Games
The organizers were prohibited from using the name "Olympics"

- San Francisco — 1,350 athletes — 1982
- San Francisco — 3,500 athletes, 40% women — 1986
- Vancouver, Canada — 7,500 athletes — 1990
- New York — 11,000 athletes — 1994
- Amsterdam — 14,700 athletes, 42% women — 1998

1896 women barred from first modern Olympic Games

0%

1900 women invited to compete in tennis, croquet, golf and yachting

1921 all women Olympic Games Jeux Feminines introduced in Monaco, and held in 1922 and 1923

4%

1928 women's track and field events introduced

10%

1936 women's gymnastics introduced

8%

16%

11%

1896 1900 1904 1908 1912 1920 1924 1928 1932 1936 1948 1952 1956 1960

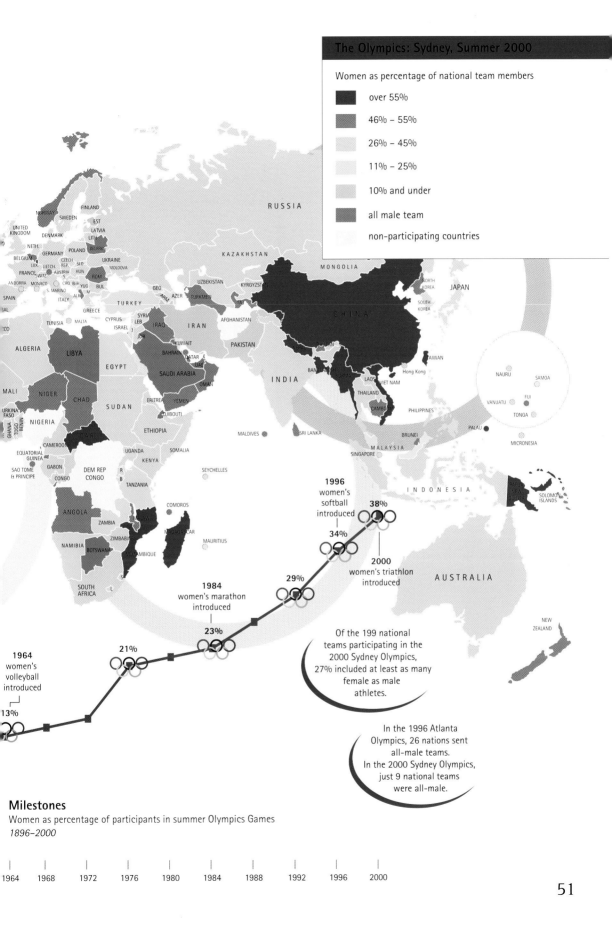

The Olympics: Sydney, Summer 2000

Women as percentage of national team members

- over 55%
- 46% – 55%
- 26% – 45%
- 11% – 25%
- 10% and under
- all male team
- non-participating countries

1964 women's volleyball introduced — 13%

1984 women's marathon introduced — 23%

1996 women's softball introduced

2000 women's triathlon introduced

21%

29%

34%

38%

Of the 199 national teams participating in the 2000 Sydney Olympics, 27% included at least as many female as male athletes.

In the 1996 Atlanta Olympics, 26 nations sent all-male teams. In the 2000 Sydney Olympics, just 9 national teams were all-male.

Milestones
Women as percentage of participants in summer Olympics Games
1896–2000

| 1964 | 1968 | 1972 | 1976 | 1980 | 1984 | 1988 | 1992 | 1996 | 2000 |

18 | Beauty

International beauty contests promote and export a white, Western standard of beauty. Globalization is accelerating the adoption of these standards around the world. As new governments seek global economic integration, they often signal this by jumping on the Western beauty bandwagon. The proliferation of beauty contests in the former Soviet bloc countries is particularly striking.

There are now few places in the world untouched by the commerce of beauty. A handful of companies control the international cosmetics market.

Women undergo a staggering amount of suffering in the pursuit of beauty. Around the world, but especially in the rich countries, tens of thousands of women each year have their bodies cut, shaped, stapled, tucked, and manipulated to conform to prevailing standards of beauty. A preoccupation with weight and body image has become an intrinsic part of the lives of women and girls. This is particularly so in the USA, but eating disorders are also noticeably increasing in Europe, Japan, and the former Soviet Union.

USA 2002
• 42% of girls in grades 1 – 3 want to be thinner.
• 81% of 10-year-old girls are afraid of being fat.
• The average US model is thinner than 98% of all US women.

Avon's world

By 2001, Avon products were on sale in 143 countries

Avon products sold

Avon opened new markets in:
1990: China, Hungary, East Germany
1991: Russia, Czechoslovakia, Panama, Ecuador, Bolivia
1992: Poland
1993: Ireland, Turkey
1996: Nicaragua, South Africa, India
1997: Ukraine, Romania, Croatia
1998: Uruguay
1999: Hong Kong, Lithuania, Slovenia, Bulgaria, Latvia
2000: Singapore, South Korea
2001: Greece Morocco

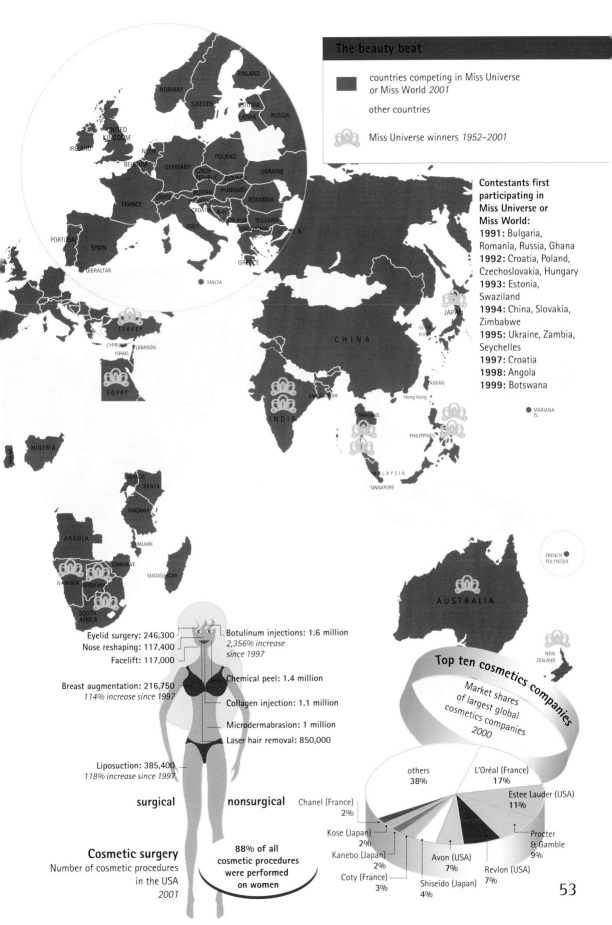

Contestants first participating in Miss Universe or Miss World:
1991: Bulgaria, Romania, Russia, Ghana
1992: Croatia, Poland, Czechoslovakia, Hungary
1993: Estonia, Swaziland
1994: China, Slovakia, Zimbabwe
1995: Ukraine, Zambia, Seychelles
1997: Croatia
1998: Angola
1999: Botswana

Eyelid surgery: 246,300
Nose reshaping: 117,400
Facelift: 117,000

Breast augmentation: 216,750
114% increase since 1997

Botulinum injections: 1.6 million
2,356% increase since 1997

Chemical peel: 1.4 million

Collagen injection: 1.1 million

Microdermabrasion: 1 million
Laser hair removal: 850,000

Liposuction: 385,400
118% increase since 1997

surgical   **nonsurgical**

Cosmetic surgery
Number of cosmetic procedures in the USA
2001

88% of all cosmetic procedures were performed on women

Top ten cosmetics companies
Market shares of largest global cosmetics companies 2000

others 38%
L'Oréal (France) 17%
Estee Lauder (USA) 11%
Procter & Gamble 9%
Avon (USA) 7%
Revlon (USA) 7%
Shiseido (Japan) 4%
Coty (France) 3%
Kanebo (Japan) 2%
Kose (Japan) 2%
Chanel (France) 2%

53

19 | Under the Knife

Female genital mutilation (FGM), also called female circumcision or genital cutting, is extensively practiced in parts of Africa and the Middle East. Its practice and prevalence varies widely across these regions and within each country, although in some places FGM is nearly universal. FGM is found in cultures representing several religions, yet it is not required by any religious teaching. An estimated 130 million girls and women in the world have undergone genital cutting; each year, another 2 million join their ranks.

FGM is mostly performed on young girls. Its over-riding purpose is to ensure the desirability and suitability of women for marriage, in large part by controlling their sexual behavior. Female genital mutilation typically reduces women's sexual desire. Infibulation is a way of ensuring premarital virginity. In some cultures female genitalia are considered unclean, and the ritual of circumcision is thought to smooth and purify girls' bodies.

FGM has severe consequences for women's physical and mental health. However, the practice is so culturally embedded in some societies that it is proving difficult to challenge. Traditionally, it is women who perform the actual cutting, and many women are strong proponents of the practice. However, it is also women who have taken the lead in organizing against FGM. Most governments remain reluctant to intervene.

Legal status of FGM where it is known to be practiced

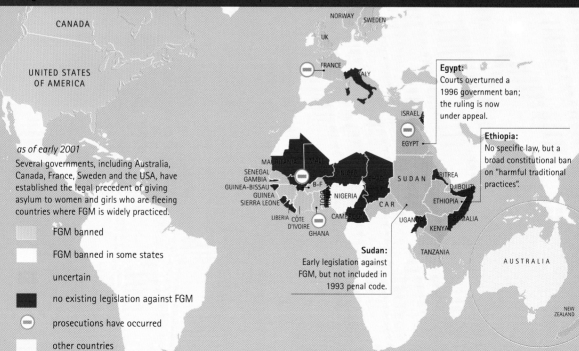

Egypt:
Courts overturned a 1996 government ban; the ruling is now under appeal.

Ethiopia:
No specific law, but a broad constitutional ban on "harmful traditional practices".

Sudan:
Early legislation against FGM, but not included in 1993 penal code.

as of early 2001
Several governments, including Australia, Canada, France, Sweden and the USA, have established the legal precedent of giving asylum to women and girls who are fleeing countries where FGM is widely practiced.

- FGM banned
- FGM banned in some states
- uncertain
- no existing legislation against FGM
- ⊖ prosecutions have occurred
- other countries

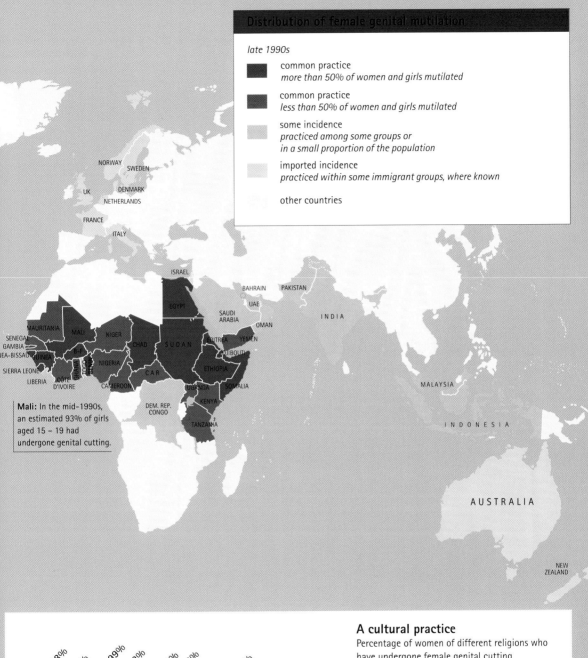

late 1990s

■ common practice
more than 50% of women and girls mutilated

■ common practice
less than 50% of women and girls mutilated

some incidence
*practiced among some groups or
in a small proportion of the population*

imported incidence
practiced within some immigrant groups, where known

other countries

NORWAY
SWEDEN
UK
DENMARK
NETHERLANDS
FRANCE
ITALY

ISRAEL
BAHRAIN   PAKISTAN
EGYPT   UAE
SAUDI
ARABIA   OMAN
INDIA

MAURITANIA   MALI   NIGER   CHAD   SUDAN   ERITREA   YEMEN
SENEGAL   DJIBOUTI
GAMBIA   B-F
GUINEA-BISSAU   GUINEA   NIGERIA   C A R   ETHIOPIA
SIERRA LEONE   GHANA   TOGO   BENIN
LIBERIA   CÔTE   CAMEROON   UGANDA   SOMALIA
D'IVOIRE   DEM. REP.   KENYA
CONGO   TANZANIA

MALAYSIA

INDONESIA

AUSTRALIA

NEW
ZEALAND

Mali: In the mid-1990s,
an estimated 93% of girls
aged 15 – 19 had
undergone genital cutting.

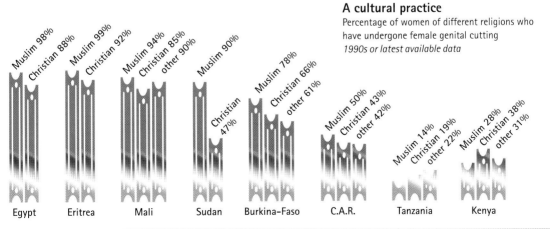

A cultural practice
Percentage of women of different religions who
have undergone female genital cutting
1990s or latest available data

Egypt — Muslim 98%, Christian 88%

Eritrea — Muslim 99%, Christian 92%

Mali — Muslim 94%, Christian 85%, other 90%

Sudan — Muslim 90%, Christian 47%

Burkina-Faso — Muslim 78%, Christian 66%, other 61%

C.A.R. — Muslim 50%, Christian 43%, other 42%

Tanzania — Muslim 14%, Christian 19%, other 22%

Kenya — Muslim 28%, Christian 38%, other 31%

20 | The Global Sex Trade

Women's bodies are commodities in the global sex trade, a multi-billion dollar industry.

The international sex trade thrives on economic disparity – between men and women at all scales, and between regions on a global scale. Globalization has heightened these disparities. New regions and countries enter into the sex trade as their economic fortunes wax or wane. As poverty deepens in Eastern Europe, it becomes a major source region for prostitutes; as wealth expands in China and Malaysia, men in those countries fuel an increased demand for the traffic in women and girls. Large circuits of trafficking operate among the countries of East and Southeast Asia, and from Central and Eastern Europe into Western Europe. The global sex trade is sustained by astounding levels of coercion, torture, rape, and systemic violence. Women are often lured into the sex trade under false pretences – hired as waitresses or maids and then forced into prostitution. Girls are often sold into prostitution by poor families and, increasingly, girls and women are simply kidnapped, often from poverty-stricken regions, to be traded globally as sex slaves and prostitutes.

The AIDS/HIV epidemic is fueling demand for younger and younger girls, as customers try to find "safe" commercial sex partners.

An estimated 50,000 women are trafficked into the USA each year.

Mail-order brides

An estimated 150,000 women are advertised each year through marriage bureaus and catalogs as being available for international marriage. There are 250 mail-order bride companies in the USA alone.

Main sending countries	Main receiving countries
China	Germany
Indonesia	Japan
Malaysia	Taiwan
Philippines	Thailand
Russia	USA
S Korea	
Thailand	
Ukraine	
Vietnam	

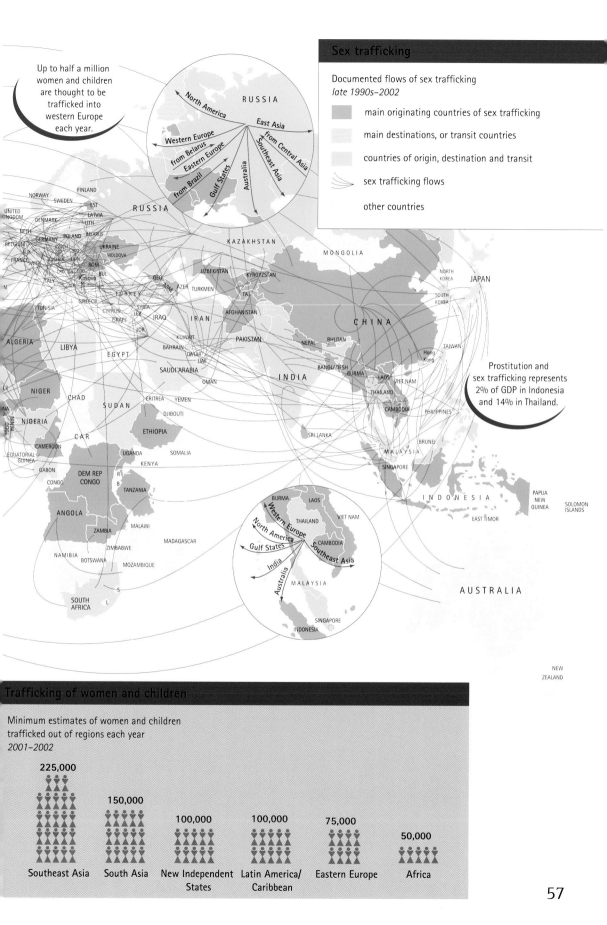

Documented flows of sex trafficking
late 1990s–2002

main originating countries of sex trafficking

main destinations, or transit countries

countries of origin, destination and transit

sex trafficking flows

other countries

Up to half a million women and children are thought to be trafficked into western Europe each year.

Prostitution and sex trafficking represents 2% of GDP in Indonesia and 14% in Thailand.

Trafficking of women and children

Minimum estimates of women and children trafficked out of regions each year
2001–2002

225,000	150,000	100,000	100,000	75,000	50,000
Southeast Asia	South Asia	New Independent States	Latin America/ Caribbean	Eastern Europe	Africa

57

21 | Rape

Women everywhere live under the threat of rape – often a threat greatest in their own homes and from men they know. In many countries, feminists are successfully changing the legal status of rape and the judicial treatment of victims to reflect the understanding that rape is not "having sex"; rape is violence intended to assert male power and control. Nonetheless, rape remains a grievously under-reported crime – because social stigma is typically attached to the victim as much as, or more than, it is to the perpetrator. Estimates suggest that the actual incidence of rape may be up to 50 times the numbers reported. In most countries, rape within marriage is not a crime.

Rape is often exercised as a "privilege" of power. Institutional rape is a widespread problem – of prisoners by jail guards and police, of patients by hospital attendants, of refugees by authorities in refugee camps. Rape in war (see Map 38) is at epidemic proportions.

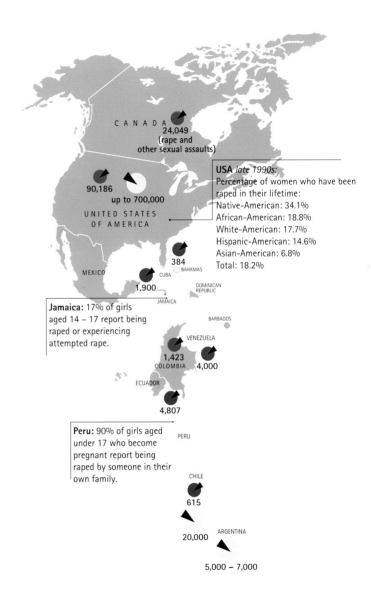

CANADA
24,049
(rape and other sexual assaults)

UNITED STATES OF AMERICA
90,186
up to 700,000

USA *late 1990s:*
Percentage of women who have been raped in their lifetime:
Native-American: 34.1%
African-American: 18.8%
White-American: 17.7%
Hispanic-American: 14.6%
Asian-American: 6.8%
Total: 18.2%

MEXICO

CUBA 384
BAHAMAS
DOMINICAN REPUBLIC
JAMAICA 1,900
BARBADOS

Jamaica: 17% of girls aged 14 – 17 report being raped or experiencing attempted rape.

VENEZUELA 4,000
COLOMBIA 1,423
ECUADOR

Peru: 90% of girls aged under 17 who become pregnant report being raped by someone in their own family.

PERU 4,807

CHILE 615

ARGENTINA 20,000
5,000 – 7,000

Child sexual abuse
Percentage of adults who report having been sexually abused as a child
1990s where known

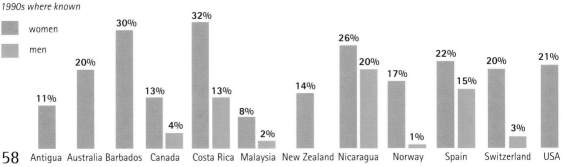

- women
- men

	women	men
Antigua	11%	
Australia	20%	
Barbados	30%	13%
Canada	13%	4%
Costa Rica	32%	13%
Malaysia	8%	2%
New Zealand	14%	
Nicaragua	26%	20%
Norway	17%	1%
Spain	22%	15%
Switzerland	20%	3%
USA	21%	

Rape

Number of rapes per year reported to police
1997 or latest available data

- number of rapes reported to the police
- actual number of rapes estimated to occur each year
- countries with marital rape laws *2000* where known

NORWAY 424
SWEDEN 1,308
FINLAND 468
ESTONIA 97
LATVIA 119
DENMARK 435
50,000
6,600 UNITED KINGDOM
IRELAND 256
166 LITHUANIA
BELARUS 577
NETH. 1,526
BELGIUM 1,694
GERMANY 6,636
CZECH REPUBLIC 655
POLAND 2,260
SLOVAKIA 173
UKRAINE 1,510
FRANCE 8,200
SWITZ.
AUSTRIA
SLOVENIA 107
HUNGARY 392
MOLDOVA 216
SPAIN
CROATIA
ITALY 1,582
ROMANIA 1,372
PORTUGAL 551
370
ALBANIA 41
BULGARIA 774
GREECE 166
RUSSIA 9,307 / 200,000

Russia: 25% of girls and 11% of boys aged 14 – 17 report unwanted sexual contact.

KAZAKHSTAN 1,687
GEORGIA 41
ARMENIA 27
AZERBAIJAN 66
TURKEY 705
CYPRUS
ISRAEL 519
JORDAN 92
KYRGYZSTAN 1,482
CHINA 40,699
SOUTH KOREA 5,327
JAPAN 1,657
PAKISTAN 2,920
INDIA 15,330
74
Hong Kong

PHILIPPINES

FIJI 103

Criminal conviction rates on charges of rape:
- Argentina: 6% – 10%
- UK: 7%;
- South Africa: 9%

Pakistan: Many women who report being raped are often then imprisoned, and some sentenced to death, for adultery or extramarital sex. An estimated 80% of women in Pakistani jails are there on adultery convictions.

THAILAND 3,726
SRI LANKA 909
MALAYSIA 1,429
SINGAPORE 103

UGANDA 268
TANZANIA 1,576
ZIMBABWE 3,900
MAURITIUS 32

NAMIBIA
SOUTH AFRICA 52,159 / 1,500,000
LESOTHO 1,080

South Africa has the highest rape rate in the world: an estimated 4,100 women a day are raped. 5% of girls and ? of boys report their first sexual experience is ?ced or coerced.

AUSTRALIA 14,353

NEW ZEALAND 804

The rapist at home

Women who say they have been subjected to sexual assault or attempted sexual assault by an intimate male partner
late 1990s

Canada	Germany	India	Nicaragua	Switzerland	UK	USA	Zimbabwe
15%	15%	28%	22%	12%	23%	15%	25%

59

Part Five
WORK

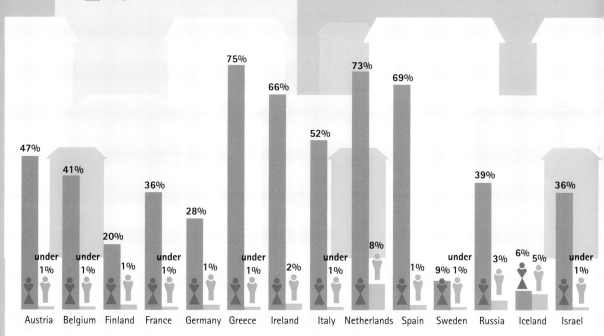

Work and family responsibilities
Percentage of women and men
who say they are not in the waged labor force
because of homemaking responsibilities
late 1990s

- women
- men

	women	men
Austria	47%	under 1%
Belgium	41%	under 1%
Finland	20%	1%
France	36%	under 1%
Germany	28%	1%
Greece	75%	under 1%
Ireland	66%	2%
Italy	52%	under 1%
Netherlands	73%	8%
Spain	69%	1%
Sweden	9%	1%
Russia	39%	3%
Iceland	6%	5%
Israel	36%	under 1%

Working for Wages

Worldwide, more and more women are working outside the home for pay, but they do so under quite different circumstances than men. They are typically paid less than men for their labor. This earnings discrepancy reflects several factors: outright gender discrimination, the concentration of women in female-dominated jobs, and the higher percentage of women working part-time. The wage gap persists across sectors. In the high-prestige, high-pay internet sector in the USA, for example, women earn 24 percent less on average than their male counterparts. Everywhere, gender differences are magnified by racial and ethnic discrimination.

Equal-pay legislation can prove effective in narrowing the earnings gap if it is seriously implemented. Even then the gender gap in wages persists because such legislation primarily dictates equal pay for the same job, but men and women typically work in different jobs ("occupational segregation").

Many women's waged work is in the informal sector – domestic service, or market trading, for example. This type of work is especially important in poorer countries and is usually a larger source of employment for women than for men.

Data on workforce participation must be treated with caution. The picture of women's work that can be drawn from official statistics is, at best, partial. What is officially counted as "work" is itself highly contested.

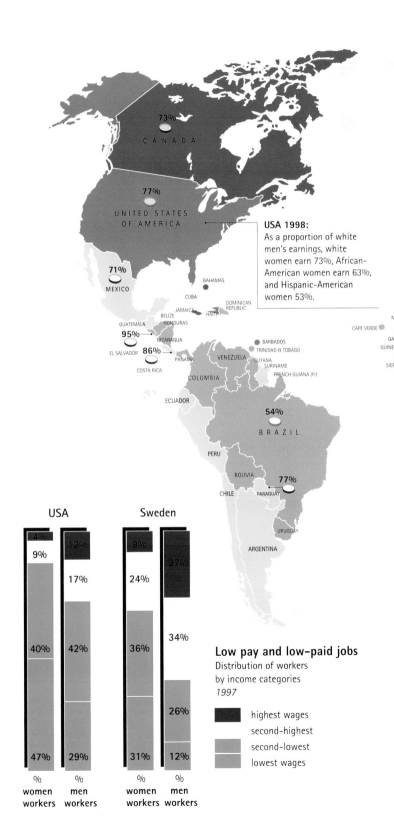

USA 1998:
As a proportion of white men's earnings, white women earn 73%, African-American women earn 63%, and Hispanic-American women 53%.

Low pay and low-paid jobs
Distribution of workers by income categories
1997

- highest wages
- second-highest
- second-lowest
- lowest wages

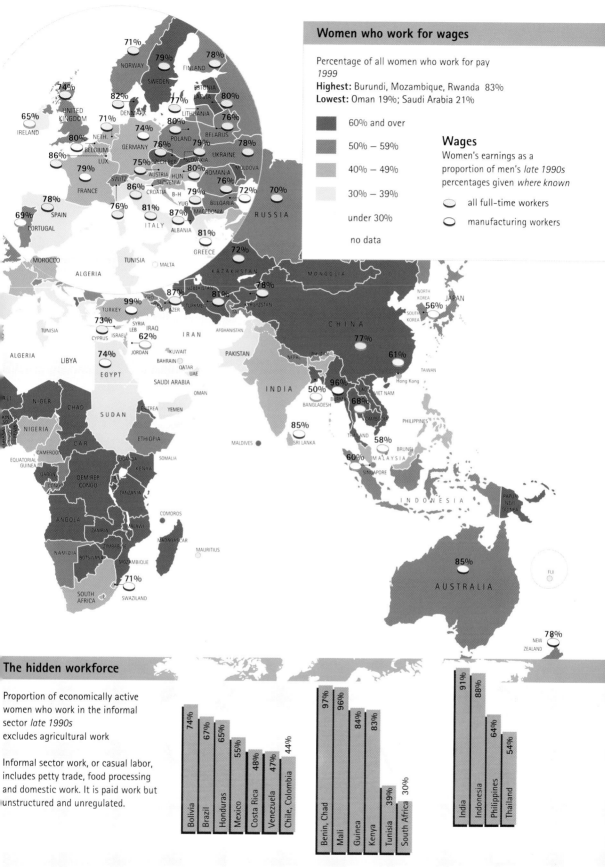

Women who work for wages

Percentage of all women who work for pay
1999
Highest: Burundi, Mozambique, Rwanda 83%
Lowest: Oman 19%; Saudi Arabia 21%

- 60% and over
- 50% – 59%
- 40% – 49%
- 30% – 39%
- under 30%
- no data

Wages

Women's earnings as a
proportion of men's *late 1990s*
percentages given *where known*

- all full-time workers
- manufacturing workers

The hidden workforce

Proportion of economically active
women who work in the informal
sector *late 1990s*
excludes agricultural work

Informal sector work, or casual labor,
includes petty trade, food processing
and domestic work. It is paid work but
unstructured and unregulated.

Bolivia 74%
Brazil 67%
Honduras 65%
Mexico 55%
Costa Rica 48%
Venezuela 47%
Chile, Colombia 44%

Benin, Chad 97%
Mali 96%
Guinea 84%
Kenya 83%
Tunisia 39%
South Africa 30%

India 91%
Indonesia 88%
Philippines 64%
Thailand 54%

23

Workplaces

Women are both "segregated" and "concentrated" in the workforce. They are employed in different occupations from men, and are over-represented in a limited number of occupations. Despite the entry of more women into the waged workforce, they are still entering the workforce in a small range of jobs. Everywhere in the world, there are "women's jobs" and "men's jobs", although the definition of these change over time and from place to place.

Generally, more women than men work in the services sector, and fewer women than men work in the industrial sector. The notable exception to this is the "global assembly line." The recent expansion of globalized industrial production – the shift of low-wage industrial production from core economies to developing countries – relies almost entirely on women's labor. Global manufacturing companies take advantage of the fact that women in poor countries have the most limited employment opportunities – and thus are the cheapest labor force available.

In the oldest Export Processing Zones (EPZs) the nature of industrial production is shifting, and the proportion of women workers is dropping: in the 1990s, about 80 percent of the employees in EPZs in Mexico and Malaysia were women; by 2000 the proportion in both countries had dropped to about 60 percent.

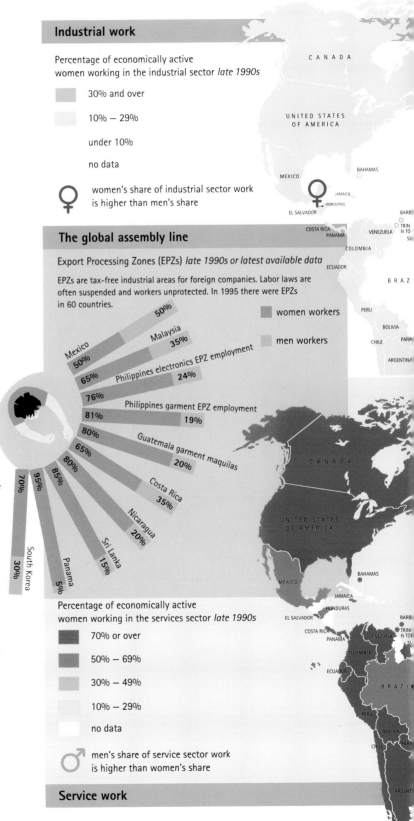

Industrial work

Percentage of economically active women working in the industrial sector *late 1990s*

- 30% and over
- 10% – 29%
- under 10%
- no data

♀ women's share of industrial sector work is higher than men's share

The global assembly line

Export Processing Zones (EPZs) *late 1990s or latest available data*

EPZs are tax-free industrial areas for foreign companies. Labor laws are often suspended and workers unprotected. In 1995 there were EPZs in 60 countries.

- women workers
- men workers

Mexico 50% 50%
Malaysia 35% 65%
Philippines electronics EPZ employment 24% 76%
Philippines garment EPZ employment 19% 81%
Guatemala garment maquilas 20% 80%
Costa Rica 35% 65%
Nicaragua 20% 80%
Sri Lanka 15% 85%
Panama 5% 95%
South Korea 30% 70%

Percentage of economically active women working in the services sector *late 1990s*

- 70% or over
- 50% – 69%
- 30% – 49%
- 10% – 29%
- no data

♂ men's share of service sector work is higher than women's share

Service work

GREENLAND

ICELAND

NORWAY FINLAND
SWEDEN
UNITED DENMARK EST
KINGDOM LATVIA
IRELAND NETH. POLAND LITH
BELGIUM GERMANY BELARUS
LUX. CZ REP. SLO
FRANCE AUS HUN MOLDOVA
S CRO
ITALY M ROM
SPAIN ARMENIA
PORTUGAL GREECE TURKEY
TUNISIA CYPRUS
ISRAEL IRAN
BAHRAIN PAKISTAN
EGYPT

RUSSIA

KYRGYZSTAN

JAPAN

SOUTH
KOREA

BANGLADESH Hong Kong
VIET NAM
THAILAND
PHILIPPINES

ETHIOPIA SRI LANKA

MALAYSIA
SINGAPORE

INDONESIA

ZIMBABWE

MAURITIUS

AUSTRALIA

NEW
ZEALAND

Europe
17% of economically active
women, and 35% of men,
work in the industrial sector.

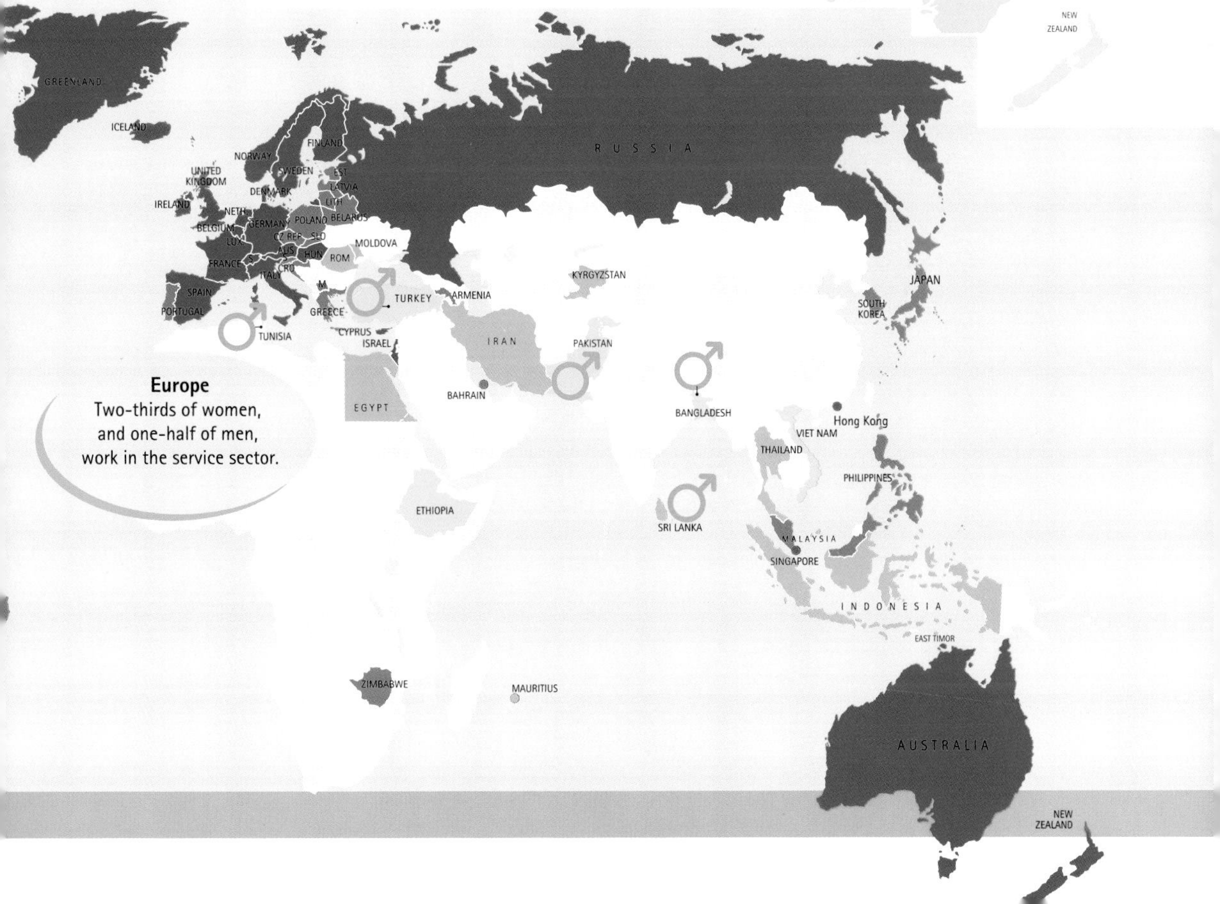

GREENLAND

ICELAND

NORWAY FINLAND
SWEDEN
UNITED DENMARK EST
KINGDOM LATVIA
IRELAND NETH. POLAND LITH
BELGIUM GERMANY BELARUS
LUX. CZ REP. SLO
FRANCE AUS HUN MOLDOVA
CRO ROM
ITALY M
SPAIN TURKEY ARMENIA
PORTUGAL GREECE
TUNISIA CYPRUS
ISRAEL IRAN PAKISTAN
BAHRAIN
EGYPT BANGLADESH

RUSSIA

KYRGYZSTAN

JAPAN

SOUTH
KOREA

Hong Kong
VIET NAM
THAILAND
PHILIPPINES

ETHIOPIA SRI LANKA

MALAYSIA
SINGAPORE

INDONESIA

EAST TIMOR

ZIMBABWE

MAURITIUS

AUSTRALIA

NEW
ZEALAND

Europe
Two-thirds of women,
and one-half of men,
work in the service sector.

24

Unequal Opportunities

The nature of women's participation in the waged labor force is shaped by many factors, including marriage, reproductive rights, and the widely prevailing expectation that women have primary responsibility for family care. Women everywhere have to balance "family" and "work" demands in ways that men seldom do. In most countries, they get little help doing so. One of the ways women manage is to work part-time; the feminization of part-time work is accelerating.

Feminists often describe women in the workforce as being "caught between the sticky floor and the glass ceiling" – concentrated in low-pay, low-status sectors on the one hand, and prevented from breaking into the top ranks on the other. Despite some modest gains in the past decade, the glass ceiling remains firmly in place. Women remain dramatically under-represented in the highest-paid, highest-prestige sectors of the workforce. Their fastest route to the top is often to start their own companies: in the USA, women-owned firms are growing at double the rate of firms owned by men.

Part time workers

Percentage of women and men aged 20 – 39 who work part-time
1998 selected countries

Women constitute about three-quarters of the world's part-time workforce

women   men

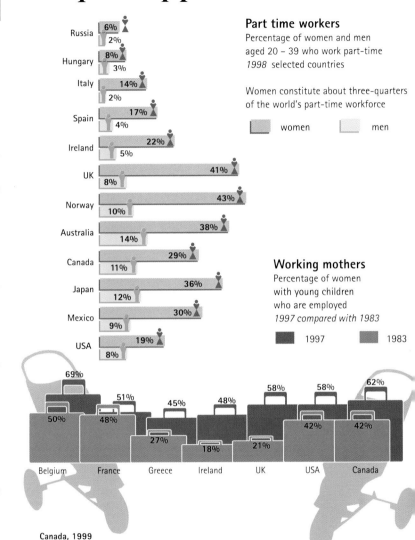

Country	Women	Men
Russia	6%	2%
Hungary	8%	3%
Italy	14%	2%
Spain	17%	4%
Ireland	22%	5%
UK	41%	8%
Norway	43%	10%
Australia	38%	14%
Canada	29%	11%
Japan	36%	12%
Mexico	30%	9%
USA	19%	8%

Working mothers

Percentage of women with young children who are employed
1997 compared with 1983

1997   1983

	1997	1983
Belgium	69%	50%
France	51%	48%
Greece	45%	27%
Ireland	48%	18%
UK	58%	21%
USA	58%	42%
Canada	62%	42%

Canada, 1999
In the 500 largest corporations, women held 12% of corporate officer positions, and only 3% of the highest positions; only 10 of the top 500 companies were run by women.

Germany, 1995
In the 70,000 largest enterprises, women held 3% of the top executive and Board Director positions.

USA, 1999
In the 500 largest corporations, women held 11% of corporate officer positions and only 5% of the most senior positions; only 3 of the top 500 companies were run by women.

Glass ceilings

Women as a percentage of "managers" in the labor force
late 1990s
developed economies

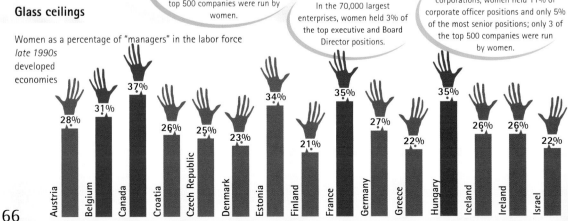

Country	%
Austria	28%
Belgium	31%
Canada	37%
Croatia	26%
Czech Republic	25%
Denmark	23%
Estonia	34%
Finland	21%
France	35%
Germany	27%
Greece	22%
Hungary	35%
Iceland	26%
Ireland	26%
Israel	22%

Maternity leave

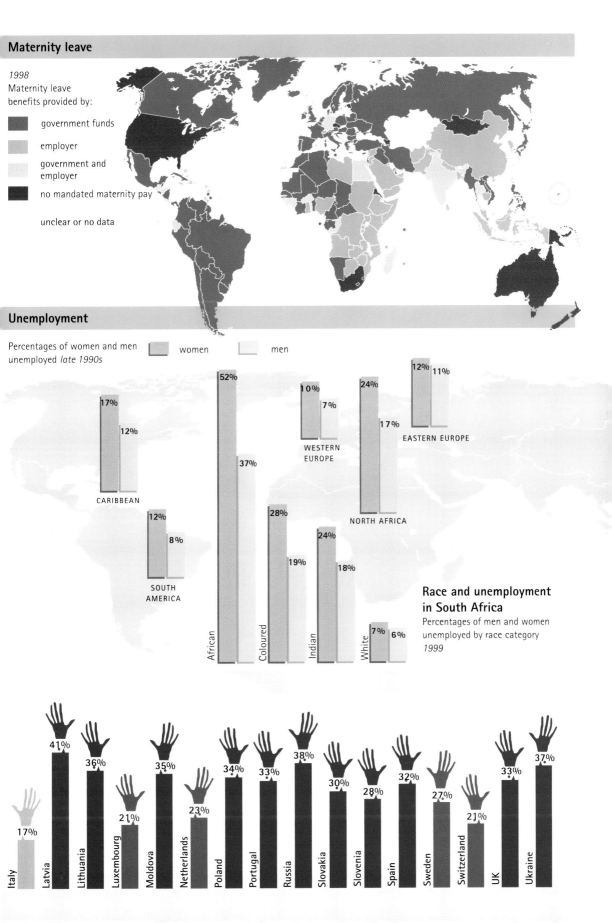

1998
Maternity leave
benefits provided by:

- government funds
- employer
- government and employer
- no mandated maternity pay
- unclear or no data

Unemployment

Percentages of women and men unemployed *late 1990s*

women   men

CARIBBEAN
17%
12%

SOUTH AMERICA
12%
8%

African
52%
37%

Coloured
28%
19%

Indian
24%
18%

White
7%
6%

WESTERN EUROPE
10%
7%

NORTH AFRICA
24%
17%

EASTERN EUROPE
12%
11%

Race and unemployment in South Africa

Percentages of men and women unemployed by race category
1999

Italy 17%
Latvia 41%
Lithuania 36%
Luxembourg 21%
Moldova 35%
Netherlands 23%
Poland 34%
Portugal 33%
Russia 38%
Slovakia 30%
Slovenia 28%
Spain 32%
Sweden 27%
Switzerland 21%
UK 33%
Ukraine 37%

The world's agricultural labor force is shrinking year by year. But as it shrinks, women make up an increasing share of the labor force that remains. In official statistics, women make up about 40 percent of the agricultural labor force worldwide – about 67 percent in developing countries. But much of women's farm work is uncounted. In most of the developing world, women grow, harvest and prepare virtually all the food consumed by their families. Much of this work is hidden under the rubric of "housework."

Modernization alters the gendered relations of agricultural production. Mechanization tends to reduce men's farm labor, but not women's: it is mostly deployed to produce cash crops, which men usually control; it opens up new economic opportunities for men, and shifts male work patterns away from home. At the same time, women's farm work increases because of the loss of men's help in subsistence production and the loss of control over crops that may have started to be profitable.

Commercialization of agriculture often reduces the land available for subsistence crop production, and leaves women to cultivate ever-more-marginal lands.

In economies where agricultural labor is paid for, women are typically employees, not employers.

95% — feeding the family
90% — fuel and water, processing
80% — storing, transporting
70% — hoeing and weeding
60% — harvesting, marketing
50% — planting, caring for livestock
30% — turning the soil
10% — hunting
5% — clearing fields

Division of labor in Africa
Percentage of agricultural tasks carried out by women in Africa *1990s*

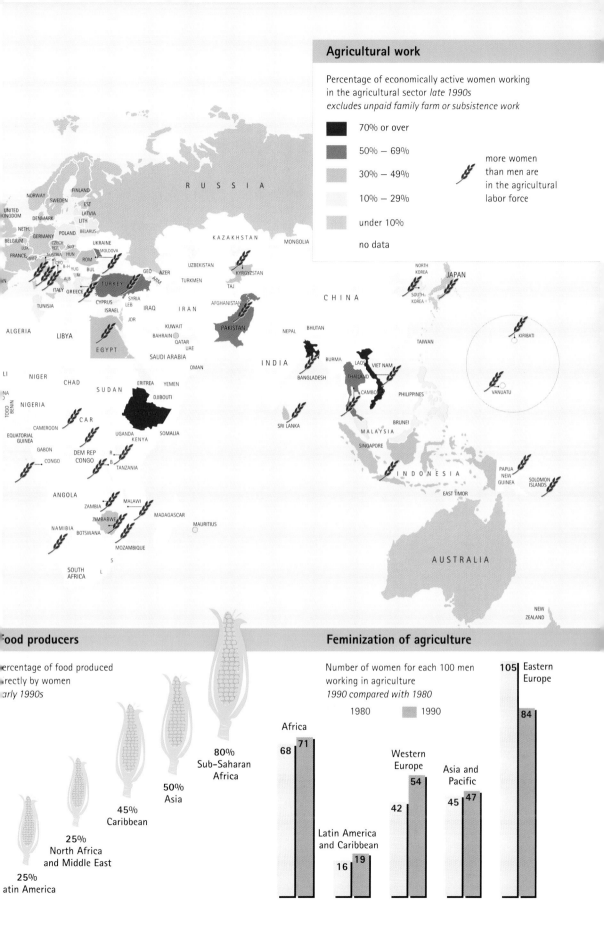

Agricultural work

Percentage of economically active women working in the agricultural sector *late 1990s*
excludes unpaid family farm or subsistence work

- 70% or over
- 50% – 69%
- 30% – 49%
- 10% – 29%
- under 10%
- no data

more women than men are in the agricultural labor force

Food producers

ercentage of food produced
rectly by women
arly 1990s

80%
Sub-Saharan
Africa

50%
Asia

45%
Caribbean

25%
North Africa
and Middle East

25%
atin America

Feminization of agriculture

Number of women for each 100 men
working in agriculture
1990 compared with 1980

1980   1990

Africa
68 | 71

**Latin America
and Caribbean**
16 | 19

**Western
Europe**
42 | 54

**Asia and
Pacific**
45 | 47

**Eastern
Europe**
105 | 84

26

Unpaid Work

Both men and women do more total "work" than conventional measurements suggest. The unpaid labor of sustaining families and households, for example, represents a substantial part of daily work that is usually overlooked in official accounts. Feminists have long pressed for an overhaul in the ways "work" is measured. One alternative way to assess the different activities of men and women is to study time use. A "time-budgets" approach to measuring men's and women's contributions to household and national productivity reveals work that is done in the informal and unpaid sector, work that is rendered invisible in official work statistics.

Time-budget studies show that women spend much more of their time than men in informal, unpaid, and household production work. Most of men's total worktime is paid, most of women's is not. Overall, women work more hours each day than men, rest less, and perform a greater variety of tasks. The pattern starts early in life: in most countries, girl children do more work, especially in the home, than boys.

Women and girls everywhere have greater responsibility for household work: it is women who tend the goats, till the family garden, collect water, shop for food, prepare meals, wash clothes, look after aging parents, and keep the home clean. A large share of women's unpaid work is household labor. Women and men who share a household often do not share household labor.

Attempts to change this allocation of household labor are at the center of personal and political struggles over gender roles, and are often fiercely resisted.

Unpaid family workers

Women as a percentage of unpaid workers in family enterprises
e.g. shops, small family businesses
late 1990s

- 80% or over
- 70% – 79%
- 50% – 69%
- 40% – 49%
- fewer than 40%
- no data

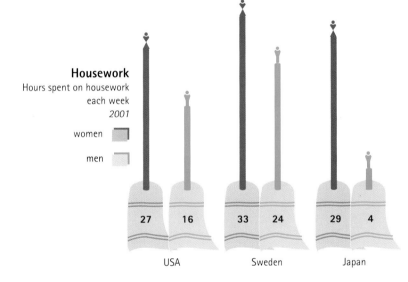

Housework
Hours spent on housework each week
2001

women

men

	USA		Sweden		Japan
	27	16	33	24	29	4

Girls and Boys
Hours per day spent reading and doing household chores
Girls and boys aged 6 to 9
rural India *averages 1990*

Reading
girls 0.4 hours
boys 2.5 hours

Household chores
girls 1.4 hours
boys 0.7 hours

India 1989–99
One survey found that women slept an average two hours less than men and spent ten times longer on household work than men; men had over two hours a day for leisure, while women had only five minutes and men spent less than one hour per week on cooking, while women spent fifteen hours per week.

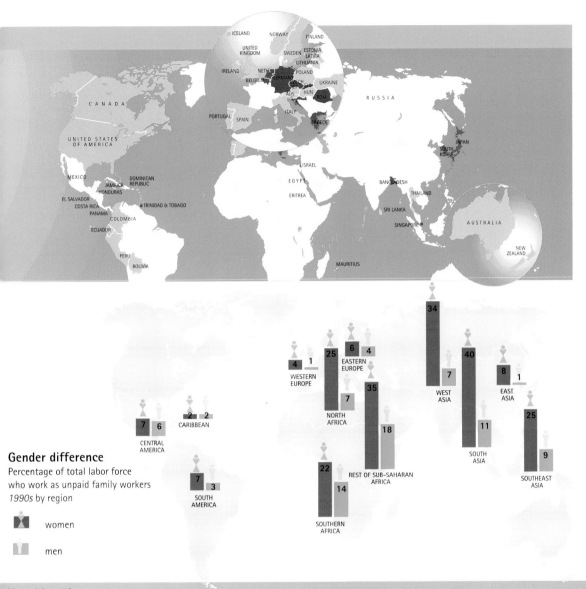

Gender difference

Percentage of total labor force
who work as unpaid family workers
1990s by region

- women
- men

Unpaid work

Percentage of time each week spent in unpaid work
1990s Europe

Worldwide 65% of women's total work time is spent doing unpaid work, such as unpaid family enterprises and housework; the average for men is about 30%. For most women, unpaid work starts at an early age.

men   women

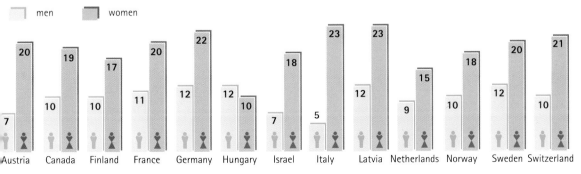

	Austria	Canada	Finland	France	Germany	Hungary	Israel	Italy	Latvia	Netherlands	Norway	Sweden	Switzerland
women	20	19	17	20	22	10	18	23	23	15	18	20	21
men	7	10	10	11	12	12	7	5	12	9	10	12	10

27

Migration

Economic globalization is accelerating the flow of migrant labor. About 100 million workers and their dependents work in countries outside their own. Asia is the largest source region of labor migrants. Every year up to 2 million Asians go overseas for jobs. Women outnumber men as migrants from the Philippines and Sri Lanka, and are a growing share of migrants from elsewhere.

Women working overseas tend to be concentrated in a few occupations, especially domestic help, labor-intensive factory production, and "entertainment". The "maid trade" is a distinct form of labor migration from poorer to richer countries. In 2002, up to 1.5 million women were working outside their own countries as foreign maids.

Some labor-exporting governments encourage out-migration, while others try to stem the tide, partly in response to publicity about the abuse of women domestics overseas. Sex traffickers (see Map 20) often lure women into their circuits by tapping into legitimate migration streams.

Labor migration from Asia
Annual outflows *late 1990s*

- Philippines 475,000
- India 450,000
- Indonesia 375,000
- Bangladesh 250,000
- Thailand 185,000
- Sri Lanka 150,000

Labor to the Middle East
Between 30,000 and 50,000 nurses and teachers a year leave India, South Korea, Sri Lanka and Philippines to work in the Middle East.

Labor around the globe
Each year about 75,000 women leave South and South East Asia to work as domestic servants, nurses, and service industry workers in Australia, Canada, the USA, and Western Europe.

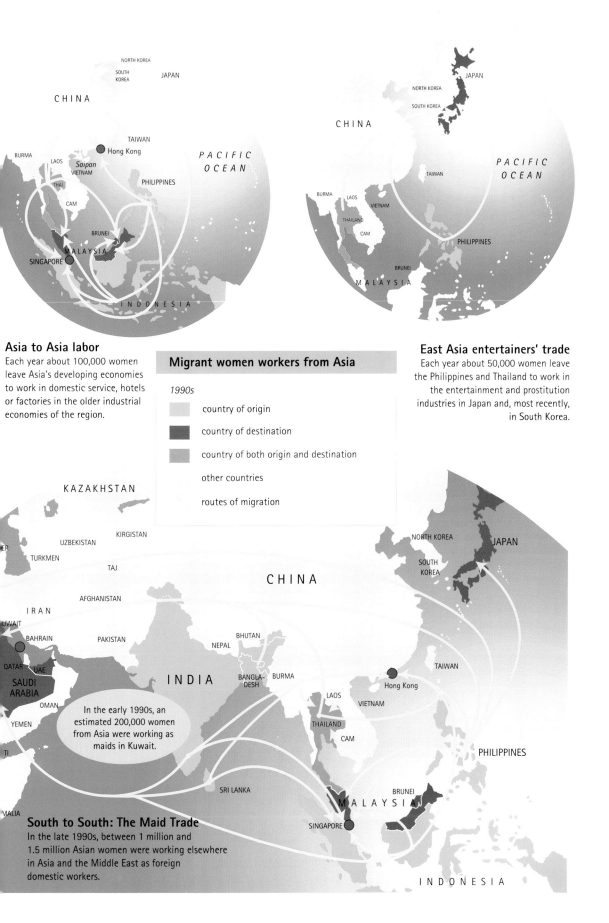

Asia to Asia labor

Each year about 100,000 women leave Asia's developing economies to work in domestic service, hotels or factories in the older industrial economies of the region.

Migrant women workers from Asia

1990s

- country of origin
- country of destination
- country of both origin and destination
- other countries
- routes of migration

East Asia entertainers' trade

Each year about 50,000 women leave the Philippines and Thailand to work in the entertainment and prostitution industries in Japan and, most recently, in South Korea.

In the early 1990s, an estimated 200,000 women from Asia were working as maids in Kuwait.

South to South: The Maid Trade

In the late 1990s, between 1 million and 1.5 million Asian women were working elsewhere in Asia and the Middle East as foreign domestic workers.

Part Six

To Have and Have Not

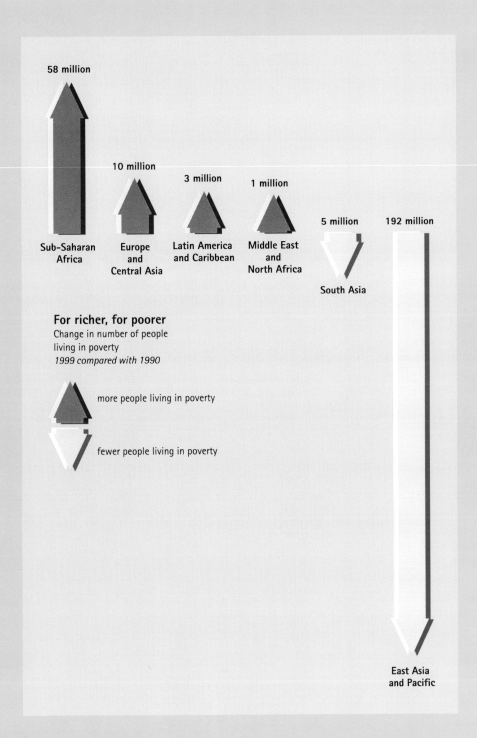

58 million

10 million

3 million

1 million

Sub-Saharan
Africa

Europe
and
Central Asia

Latin America
and Caribbean

Middle East
and
North Africa

5 million

South Asia

192 million

For richer, for poorer
Change in number of people
living in poverty
1999 compared with 1990

more people living in poverty

fewer people living in poverty

East Asia
and Pacific

Nearly a billion people in the world are illiterate, about two-thirds of whom are women.

Generalized illiteracy is mostly a function of poverty and limited educational opportunity. Higher rates of illiteracy for women, however, also suggest entrenched gender discrimination. Some of the gender-specific factors that produce high rates of women's illiteracy include: the time overburdening of women, especially in rural areas (Map 25); the restriction of girls and women to the domestic sphere; and resistance from men who fear losing their domestic power if women become literate. Illiteracy diminishes women's economic well-being, increases their dependency on men, reinforces their ties to the domestic sphere, and diminishes their ability to control or understand their own property, wealth, health, and legal rights.

The good news is that worldwide illiteracy rates have been steadily declining over the past three decades, largely the result of efforts to increase basic educational opportunities for girls.

Global figures on illiteracy generally do not incorporate information on "functional illiteracy," which is actually growing in many of the world's richest countries. In these countries, the literacy pattern is reversed – women tend to have lower rates of functional illiteracy than men. This reflects the growing "feminization" of education (Map 30) in the post-industrial rich world.

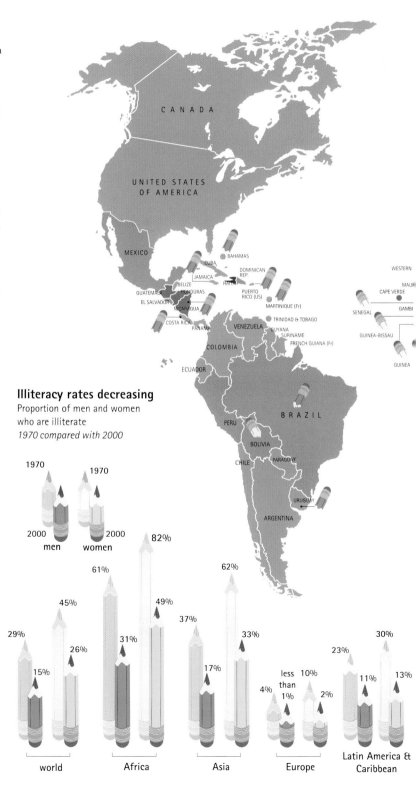

Illiteracy rates decreasing
Proportion of men and women who are illiterate
1970 compared with 2000

Illiteracy

Percentage of adult women who are illiterate
2000

Highest: Niger 92%; Burkina Faso 87%; Afghanistan 80%

- over 75%
- 51% – 75%
- 26% – 50%
- 11% – 25%
- 10% and under
- no data

illiteracy rate of women
20 or more percentage points
higher than men's

illiteracy rate of men
marginally higher
than women's

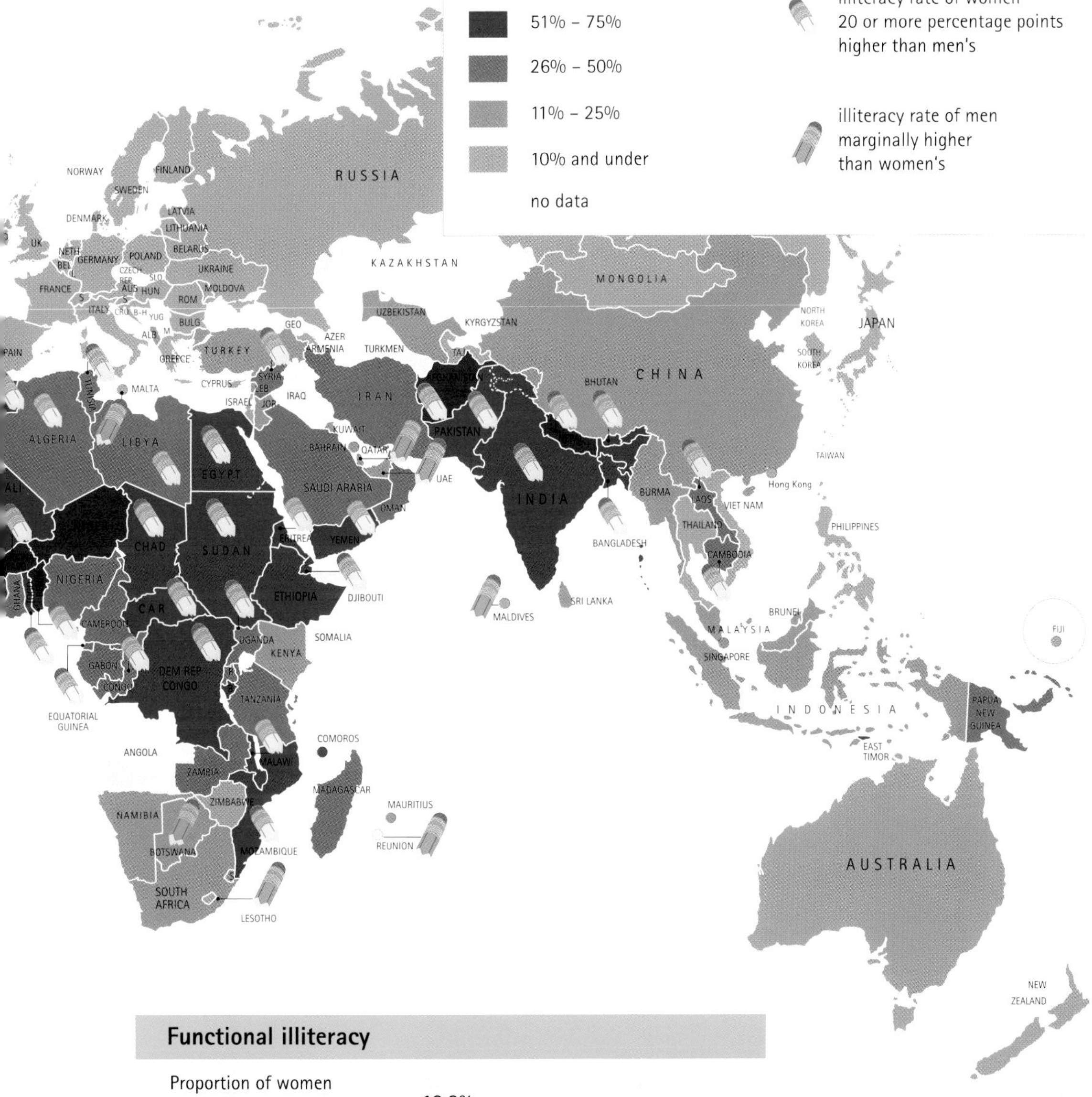

Functional illiteracy

Proportion of women
with lowest levels
of literacy skills
1994 percentages

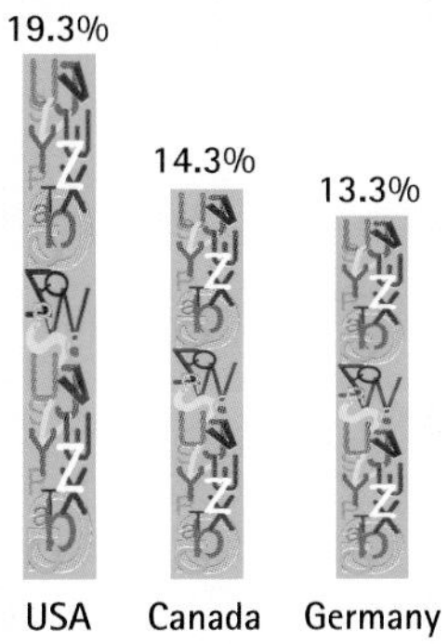

19.3%
14.3%
13.3%

USA   Canada   Germany

More girls are in primary school than ever before, and more of them are staying in school longer. In many parts of the world, boy and girl primary school enrolments are now equal or almost equal. This significant advance in girls' education is the result of concerted international and national efforts to remove restrictive legislation, to enforce equally any existing mandatory-schooling legislation, and to educate parents about the importance of educating girls.

However, it is still the case that proportionally fewer girls are enrolled in school than boys, and they are removed from school at an earlier age. Girls are still held back by presumptions that educating them will be a "waste," that they should be primarily in the home not in the workplace, and that girls are less capable than boys. The biggest gaps between boy and girl enrolment rates are found in Sub-Saharan Africa. In several countries, the average number of years of total schooling for girls remains below one full year.

Despite the generally positive global trends, progress made in girls' school enrolment has proved tenuous. Girls' enrolment rates have declined in the past decade in several countries where war, economic hardship, and declining international donor assistance makes their education seem a luxury that cannot be afforded in hard times.

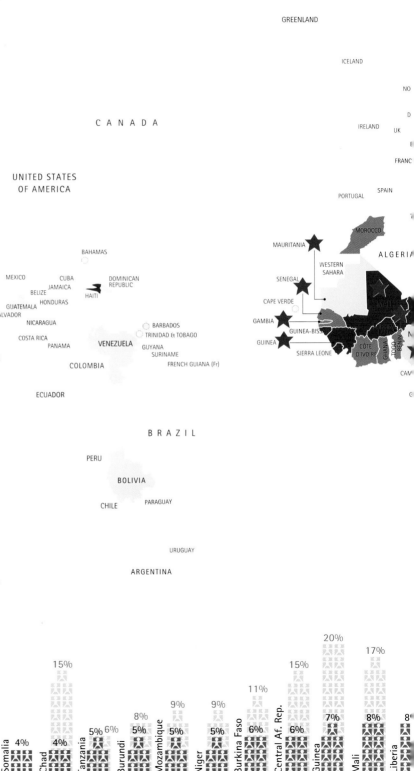

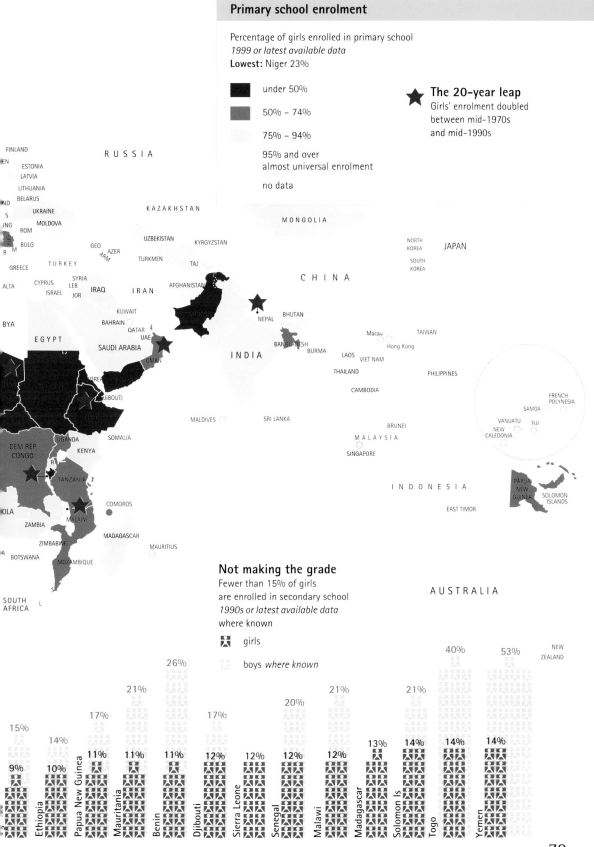

Primary school enrolment

Percentage of girls enrolled in primary school
1999 or latest available data
Lowest: Niger 23%

under 50%

50% – 74%

75% – 94%

95% and over
almost universal enrolment

no data

The 20-year leap
Girls' enrolment doubled
between mid-1970s
and mid-1990s

FINLAND
EN
ESTONIA
LATVIA
LITHUANIA
ND   BELARUS
S   UKRAINE
JNG   MOLDOVA
      ROM
YUG
B M BULG
GREECE   TURKEY
ALTA CYPRUS SYRIA
      ISRAEL LEB
              JOR IRAQ
BYA   BAHRAIN
EGYPT   SAUDI ARABIA
         QATAR
         UAE
         OMAN
        YEMEN
        ERITREA
        DJIBOUTI
        ETHIOPIA
GAR
        SOMALIA
DEM REP UGANDA
CONGO   KENYA
R
TANZANIA
OLA   COMOROS
ZAMBIA   MALAWI
ZIMBABWE   MADAGASCAR
BOTSWANA   MAURITIUS
MOZAMBIQUE
SOUTH
AFRICA L

RUSSIA

KAZAKHSTAN

UZBEKISTAN KYRGYZSTAN
GEO AZER
ARM
TURKMEN   TAJ
AFGHANISTAN
PAKISTAN

KUWAIT

INDIA

MALDIVES   SRI LANKA

MONGOLIA

NORTH
KOREA   JAPAN
SOUTH
KOREA

CHINA

NEPAL BHUTAN
BANGLADESH
        BURMA Macau TAIWAN
LAOS   Hong Kong
VIET NAM
THAILAND
CAMBODIA
              PHILIPPINES
BRUNEI
MALAYSIA
SINGAPORE

INDONESIA

EAST TIMOR

FRENCH
POLYNESIA
SAMOA
VANUATU FIJI
NEW
CALEDONIA

PAPUA
NEW
GUINEA   SOLOMON
         ISLANDS

Not making the grade
Fewer than 15% of girls
are enrolled in secondary school
1990s or latest available data
where known

girls

boys *where known*

AUSTRALIA

NEW
ZEALAND

		26%											40%	53%	
		21%	17%					21%	21%						
	17%					20%									
15%	14%														
		11% 11% 11%	12%	12% 12%	12%		13% 14%	14%	14%					
9% 10%															

Ethiopia | Papua New Guinea | Mauritania | Benin | Djibouti | Sierra Leone | Senegal | Malawi | Madagascar | Solomon Is | Togo | Yemen

79

30

Higher Education

Worldwide, more and more women are going on to higher education, although in most countries it is still a preserve of the elite. In many industrialized countries, women now represent a slight majority of all university students. Ironically, as this trend has been identified it has immediately been labeled as worrisome: social analysts are starting to warn against the "feminization of education" and the apparent alienation of men from schooling. The proportional representation of women in university faculties has not increased at a concomitant pace.

There continue to be significant gender differences in the subjects studied and degrees taken. Women remain dramatically under represented among students and faculty in the sciences, and in technology and engineering.

Universities started to admit women in the late 19th century, often after vociferous resistance. In many countries, the gates did not open to women until the 1950s or 1960s. At most of the world's most prestigious universities there were large gaps between when they were founded and when women were admitted: 711 years at Oxford, 589 years at Cambridge, 258 years at Harvard.

University attendance is not always the most important tertiary schooling. In many countries, other third level institutions such as teachers' colleges offer the most important educational opportunities to women.

USA
25 to 29 year-olds completing four years or more of college:
white women: 35%
white men: 32%
Black women: 17%
Black men: 13%
Hispanic women: 10%
Hispanic men: 8%

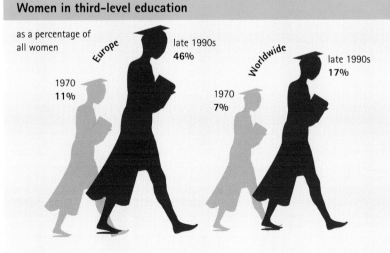

Women in third-level education

as a percentage of all women

Europe
late 1990s
46%
1970
11%

Worldwide
late 1990s
17%
1970
7%

University students

Women as a percentage of university students
mid–1990s or latest available data
Highest: Cyprus 75%

- 60% and over
- 40% – 59%
- 20% – 39%
- under 20%
- no data

Sub-Saharan Africa
Only 2 out of every 1,000 women and 4 out of 1,000 men have access to higher education.

20–39%

Bahrain, Iran, Mozambique, Uganda 21%
Japan, Morocco 22%
Gambia 23%
Algeria, Cambodia 24%
Germany 25%
Mauritius 26%
Austria, Tunisia 27%
Botswana, Colombia, South Korea 28%
El Salvador, Guyana, Honduras, Italy, Madagascar, Saudi Arabia 29%
Albania, Denmark, Egypt, Malawi, UK 30%
Hungary, Ireland 31%
Dominican Republic, Spain, Swaziland 32%
Greece, Lebanon, Qatar, Sri Lanka, Turkey 33%
Australia, Canada, Croatia, France, Georgia, Laos, Viet Nam 34%
Romania, Sweden 35%
Norway 36%
South Africa 37%
Brazil, Nicaragua 38%
Bulgaria, USA 39%

40% and over

Macedonia 41%
Estonia, Moldova, New Zealand 42%
Mongolia 43%
Cuba 45%
Latvia, St Lucia 49%
Czech Republic 52%

Women as a percentage of all university teachers

1990s or latest available data
selected countries

2%–19%

Burkina Faso 2%
Guinea 4%
Ethiopia 6%
Congo Rep. 8%
Togo 10%
Burundi 11%
Benin, Tanzania 12%
Eritrea, Jordan 13%
Kuwait, Switzerland 14%
Syria, Zimbabwe 16%

31

Wired Women

The internet is a powerful agent of social change, but only about one percent of the world's people have access to it. The "digital divide" is found locally and globally – along race, class, age and gender lines. More than 80 percent of internet users are in the industrialized countries; Africa is the least wired.

Most of the world's internet users are male, higher-income, and urban. However, where the technology is most widely diffused, the gender gap is rapidly closing. Women often first learn skills and gain access to the internet in the workplace.

The internet offers great potential as a tool of political liberation. Women's groups have been fast to adopt the technology; women's websites proliferate. Unfortunately, it also offers new venues for sexual exploitation. Pornography flourishes on the Web, and it has facilitated global trafficking in women and children.

In 2001, 41% of gay and lesbian internet users in Europe booked travel online, compared with 28% of heterosexual users.

In 2000, women made up only 28% of computer science graduates in the USA; in 1984, they were 37%.

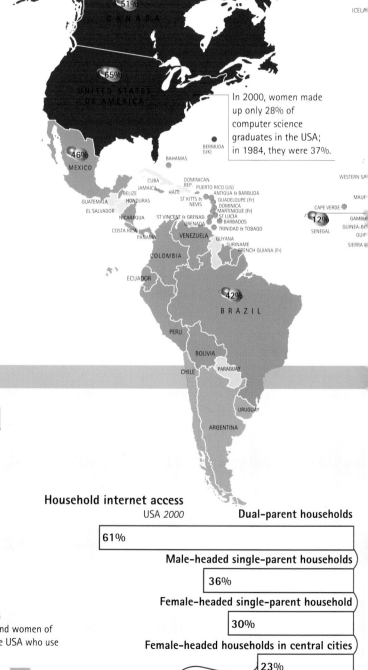

Digital Divide USA

Asian
72%
60%

White
55%
50%

Hispanic
48%
45%

African-American
38%
37%

Gender matters
Proportion of men and women of different races in the USA who use the internet 2001

men   women

Household internet access
USA *2000*

Dual-parent households
61%

Male-headed single-parent households
36%

Female-headed single-parent household
30%

Female-headed households in central cities
23%

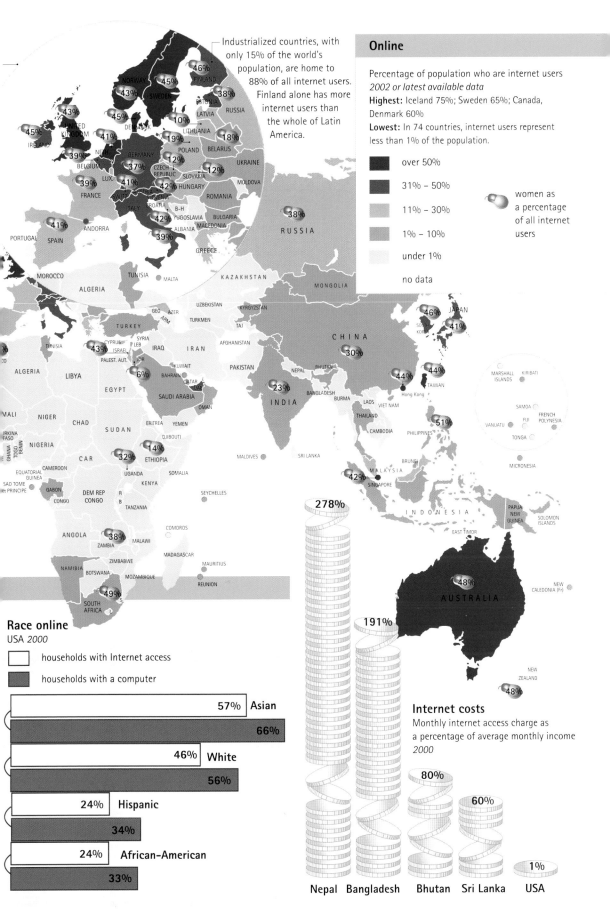

Industrialized countries, with only 15% of the world's population, are home to 88% of all internet users. Finland alone has more internet users than the whole of Latin America.

Online

Percentage of population who are internet users
2002 or latest available data
Highest: Iceland 75%; Sweden 65%; Canada, Denmark 60%
Lowest: In 74 countries, internet users represent less than 1% of the population.

- over 50%
- 31% – 50%
- 11% – 30%
- 1% – 10%
- under 1%
- no data

women as a percentage of all internet users

Map labels (women as a percentage of all internet users):
NORWAY 43%, SWEDEN 45%, FINLAND 46%, ESTONIA 38%, LATVIA 10%, RUSSIA, UNITED KINGDOM 43%, IRELAND 45%, DENMARK 41%, LITHUANIA 19%, POLAND 12%, BELARUS 18%, NETH. 39%, GERMANY 37%, CZECH REPUBLIC, SLOVAKIA 12%, UKRAINE, HUNGARY 12%, MOLDOVA, BELGIUM, LUX. 39%, SWITZ. 41%, AUSTRIA 42%, ROMANIA, FRANCE, ITALY, CROATIA, SLOVENIA, B-H, YUGOSLAVIA 42%, BULGARIA, MACEDONIA, ALBANIA 39%, RUSSIA 38%, SPAIN 41%, PORTUGAL, ANDORRA, GREECE

ISRAEL 43%, PALEST. AUT. 6%, JAPAN 46%, SOUTH KOREA 41%, CHINA 30%, TAIWAN 44%, Hong Kong 44%, INDIA 23%, PHILIPPINES 51%, ETHIOPIA 14%, 32%, ZAMBIA 38%, SOUTH AFRICA 49%, MALAYSIA/SINGAPORE 42%, AUSTRALIA 48%, NEW ZEALAND 48%

Race online
USA *2000*

- □ households with Internet access
- ■ households with a computer

	Internet access	Computer
Asian	57%	66%
White	46%	56%
Hispanic	24%	34%
African-American	24%	33%

Internet costs
Monthly internet access charge as a percentage of average monthly income
2000

Nepal	Bangladesh	Bhutan	Sri Lanka	USA
278%	191%	80%	60%	1%

The majority of the world's women do not equally own, inherit, or control property, land and wealth. Discriminatory legal inheritance and property ownership laws are still widely in effect around the world.

Property discrimination in agrarian economies is particularly striking – women typically work the fields, prepare, grow and harvest the food (see Map 25) , but cannot own the land. Land and property provide leverage for other economic advantages. For example, land is typically required as collateral for loans; if women do not own or control land, they cannot get credit.

In industrialized countries, there is a similar pecking order for homeownership, with fewer women than men owning homes. In most industrialized countries as recently as the mid-1970s gender-based discrimination in mortgages, credit, and loans was entirely legal and widely entrenched.

Even where there is no legal discrimination, women are subject to social pressures or economic realities that create unequal access to land, property and wealth. For example, they are pressured to turn over property or financial matters to male relatives, they are pressured not to exercise their full inheritance rights, and they are socialized to believe that financial matters are beyond their realm.

Globalization has tended to deepen women's property disadvantage as the cash economy has displaced communal or household-based land use.

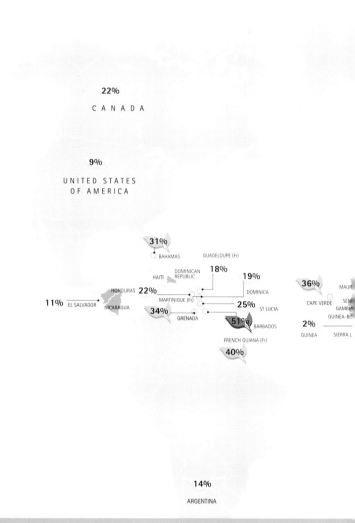

Home ownership in the USA

Percentage of households
who own their own homes *2001*

USA average (all races): 68%

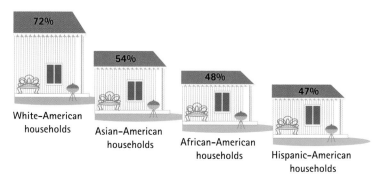

72% White–American households

54% Asian–American households

48% African–American households

47% Hispanic–American households

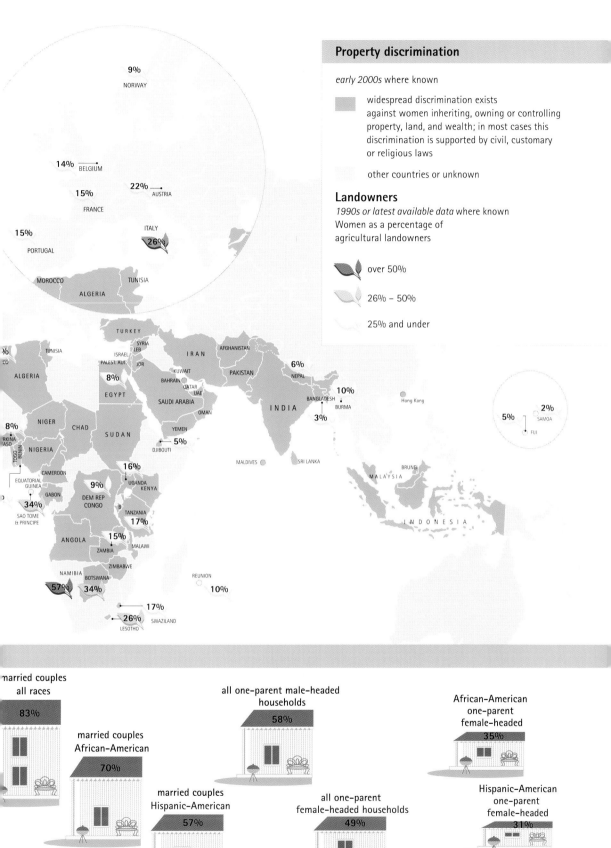

Property discrimination

early 2000s where known

widespread discrimination exists
against women inheriting, owning or controlling
property, land, and wealth; in most cases this
discrimination is supported by civil, customary
or religious laws

other countries or unknown

Landowners
1990s or latest available data where known
Women as a percentage of
agricultural landowners

over 50%

26% – 50%

25% and under

Map labels:

9% NORWAY

14% BELGIUM

15% FRANCE

22% AUSTRIA

26% ITALY

15% PORTUGAL

MOROCCO

ALGERIA

TUNISIA

TURKEY

SYRIA
LEB

ISRAEL
PALEST. AUT.
JOR

IRAN

AFGHANISTAN

6% NEPAL

TUNISIA

CO

ALGERIA

KUWAIT

BAHRAIN
QATAR
UAE

PAKISTAN

8% EGYPT

SAUDI ARABIA

OMAN

INDIA

10% BANGLADESH
BURMA

3%

Hong Kong

2% SAMOA

5%

FIJI

8%

RKINA
ASO

NIGER

CHAD

SUDAN

YEMEN

5% DJIBOUTI

TOGO
BENIN

NIGERIA

CAMEROON

MALDIVES

SRI LANKA

BRUNEI

MALAYSIA

EQUATORIAL
GUINEA

GABON

16% UGANDA
KENYA

34%
SAO TOME
& PRINCIPE

9% DEM REP
CONGO

B

TANZANIA
17%

INDONESIA

ANGOLA

15% ZAMBIA

MALAWI

ZIMBABWE

NAMIBIA

BOTSWANA

57%

34%

REUNION

10%

17%

26% SWAZILAND
LESOTHO

Bottom chart — home ownership:

married couples
all races
83%

married couples
African-American
70%

married couples
Hispanic-American
57%

all one-parent male-headed
households
58%

all one-parent
female-headed households
49%

African-American
one-parent
female-headed
35%

Hispanic-American
one-parent
female-headed
31%

Poverty

The majority of the world's population is poor. Women are the majority of the world's poor. The poorest of the poor are women. More so than men, women lack the resources either to stave off poverty in the first place, or to climb out of poverty – they have limited ownership of income, property, and credit. Women not only bear the brunt of poverty, they bear the brunt of "managing" poverty: as providers and caretakers of their families, it is women's labor and women's personal austerity that typically compensate for diminished resources of the family or household.

Official poverty rates underestimate actual deprivation, and "poverty" is hard to measure. What is clear, though, is that since the early 1990s the gulf between rich and poor has widened dramatically on scales from the global to the local. The total income of the richest one percent of the people in the world is now about the same as the total income of the poorest 60 percent.

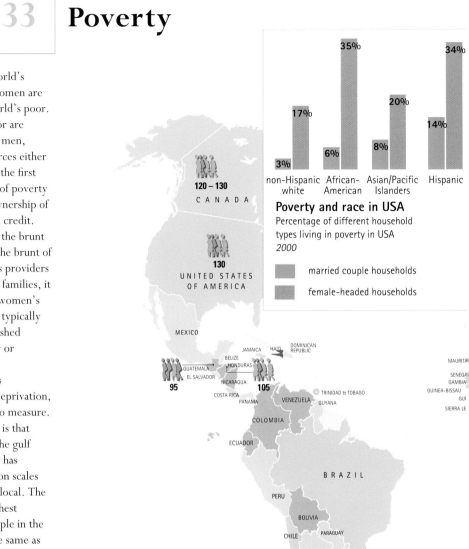

Poverty and race in USA
Percentage of different household types living in poverty in USA
2000

- married couple households
- female-headed households

	non-Hispanic white	African-American	Asian/Pacific Islanders	Hispanic
married couple households	3%	6%	8%	14%
female-headed households	17%	35%	20%	34%

Income inequality

The GINI coefficient measures inequality across income distribution to show the inequality gap between rich and poor within a country.

- high income inequality
- moderate degree of inequality across incomes
- relatively even distribution of income

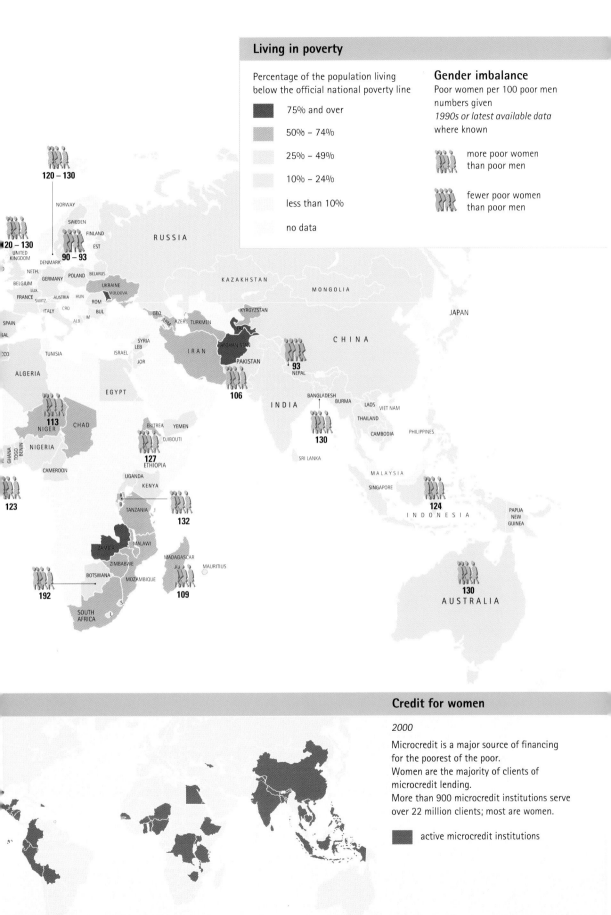

120 – 130

NORWAY

SWEDEN

FINLAND

EST

RUSSIA

20 – 130
UNITED
KINGDOM

90 – 93

DENMARK

NETH.

BELGIUM
LUX.
FRANCE
SWITZ.
AUSTRIA HUN
ITALY CRO
ALB

GERMANY POLAND BELARUS

UKRAINE
MOLDOVA

ROM

BUL

KAZAKHSTAN

MONGOLIA

SPAIN

IAL

CCO

TUNISIA

ISRAEL

SYRIA
LEB
JOR

GEO
ARM
AZER TURKMEN

IRAN

AFGHANISTAN

PAKISTAN

106

KYRGYZSTAN

CHINA

JAPAN

93
NEPAL

ALGERIA

EGYPT

BANGLADESH
INDIA

BURMA

LAOS
VIET NAM

113
NIGER

CHAD

ERITREA YEMEN

DJIBOUTI

THAILAND

CAMBODIA

PHILIPPINES

130

GHANA
TOGO
BENIN

NIGERIA

CAMEROON

127
ETHIOPIA

SRI LANKA

MALAYSIA

SINGAPORE

123

UGANDA
KENYA

R
B

TANZANIA

132

124

INDONESIA

PAPUA
NEW
GUINEA

ZAMBIA

MALAWI

ZIMBABWE

BOTSWANA

MOZAMBIQUE

MADAGASCAR

MAURITIUS

109

130

AUSTRALIA

192

S.

SOUTH
AFRICA

34

Debt

Women are the "shock-absorbers" of economic crises. When governments cut back spending on social and health services to cope with their debt burden, poor households, of which women-headed households are a disproportionate share, bear the brunt of these cuts. Women's labor keeps households going.

Economic adjustment programs imposed by the IMF and World Bank on governments in exchange for loans have deepened poverty and increased social inequities. Most Eastern European, African and Latin American governments are now heavily in debt. Under great pressure from critics, the World Bank has now started to develop "poverty alleviation" programs. Critics say it is too little, too late.

Poverty versus power
2002
- 70% of the world's poor are women
- There are no women on the IMF Board of Directors
- 8% of the World Bank Directors are women
- 2% of IMF Governers are women
- 6% of World Bank Governors are women

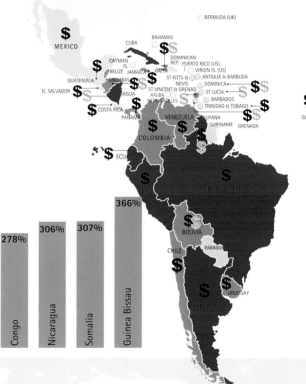

External debt compared with GNP
Debt as percentage of GNP
late 1990s
selected countries

Country	%
Ethiopia	159%
Sudan	182%
Zambia	185%
DR Congo	232%
Mauritania	235%
Mozambique	249%
Congo	278%
Nicaragua	306%
Somalia	307%
Guinea Bissau	366%

Regional trends
External debt as a percentage of GNP
1997 compared with 1985

1985   1997

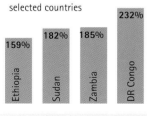

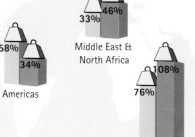

Americas 58% / 34%
Middle East & North Africa 33% / 46%
Sub-Saharan Africa 76% / 108%
East and South Asia / Pacific 29% / 33%

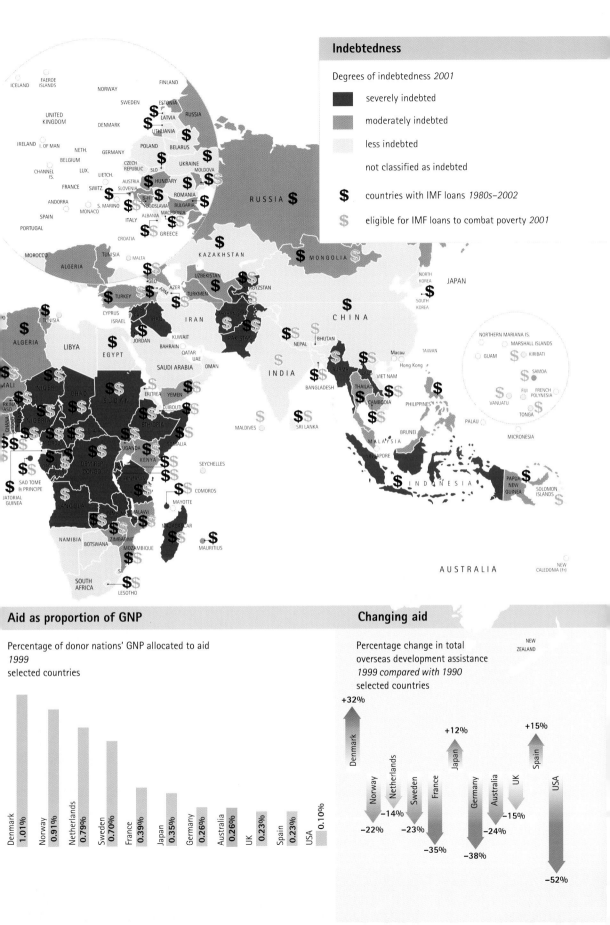

Indebtedness

Degrees of indebtedness *2001*

- severely indebted
- moderately indebted
- less indebted
- not classified as indebted

$ countries with IMF loans *1980s–2002*

$ eligible for IMF loans to combat poverty *2001*

Aid as proportion of GNP

Percentage of donor nations' GNP allocated to aid
1999
selected countries

Country	%
Denmark	1.01%
Norway	0.91%
Netherlands	0.79%
Sweden	0.70%
France	0.39%
Japan	0.35%
Germany	0.26%
Australia	0.26%
UK	0.23%
Spain	0.23%
USA	0.10%

Changing aid

Percentage change in total
overseas development assistance
1999 compared with 1990
selected countries

- Denmark +32%
- Norway −22%
- Netherlands −14%
- Sweden −23%
- France +12%
- Germany −38%
- Australia −24%
- UK −15%
- Spain +15%
- USA −52%

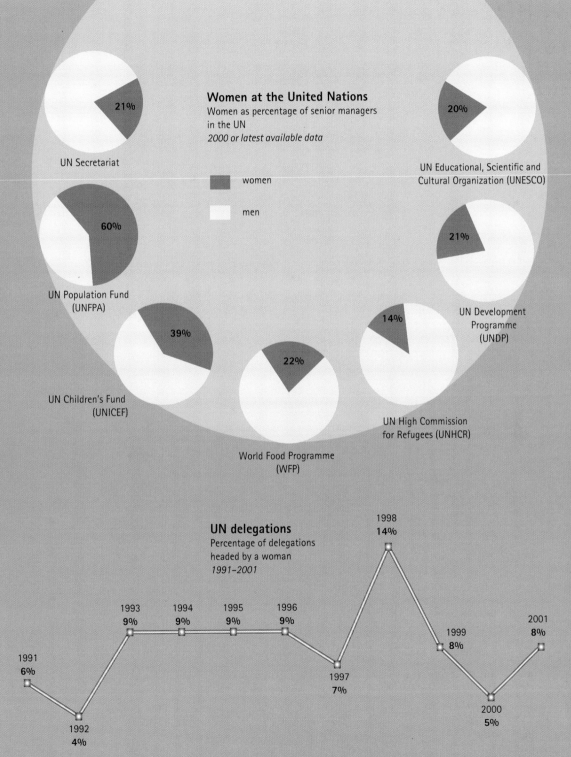

Women at the United Nations
Women as percentage of senior managers
in the UN
2000 or latest available data

women

men

UN Secretariat

UN Educational, Scientific and
Cultural Organization (UNESCO)

21%

20%

UN Population Fund
(UNFPA)

60%

UN Development
Programme
(UNDP)

21%

UN Children's Fund
(UNICEF)

39%

UN High Commission
for Refugees (UNHCR)

14%

World Food Programme
(WFP)

22%

UN delegations
Percentage of delegations
headed by a woman
1991–2001

1998
14%

1993
9%

1994
9%

1995
9%

1996
9%

1999
8%

2001
8%

1991
6%

1997
7%

1992
4%

2000
5%

35

The Vote

In most countries, men gained the right to vote before women did. Almost everywhere, voting rights for women were resisted, sometimes fiercely.

For most countries, it is difficult to identify a single date when women won the vote. This right was often doled out in stages, and restricted suffrage was common. Typically some women – such as married women, literate women, or the wives of soldiers – were granted the vote before others. In colonized countries, women of the colonizing class almost always had the vote before indigenous women did.

In reality, the right to vote does not ensure the exercise of that right. Many governments restrict or entirely prevent anyone from voting.

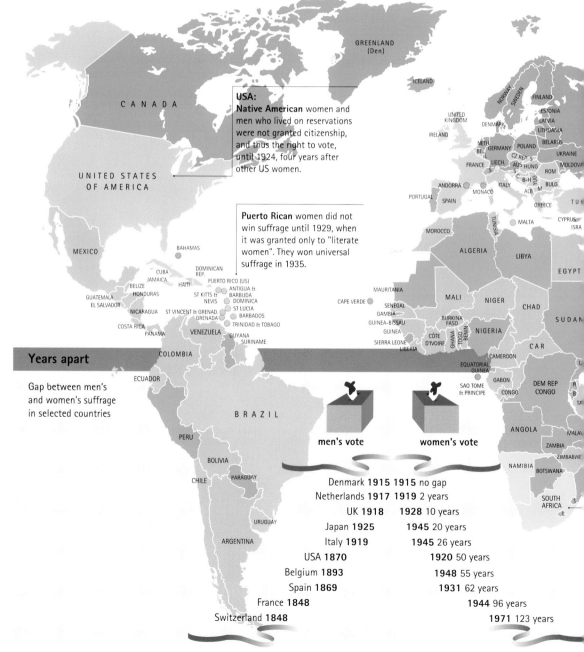

USA:
Native American women and men who lived on reservations were not granted citizenship, and thus the right to vote, until 1924, four years after other US women.

Puerto Rican women did not win suffrage until 1929, when it was granted only to "literate women". They won universal suffrage in 1935.

Years apart

Gap between men's and women's suffrage in selected countries

men's vote   women's vote

	men's vote	women's vote	gap
Denmark	1915	1915	no gap
Netherlands	1917	1919	2 years
UK	1918	1928	10 years
Japan	1925	1945	20 years
Italy	1919	1945	26 years
USA	1870	1920	50 years
Belgium	1893	1948	55 years
Spain	1869	1931	62 years
France	1848	1944	96 years
Switzerland	1848	1971	123 years

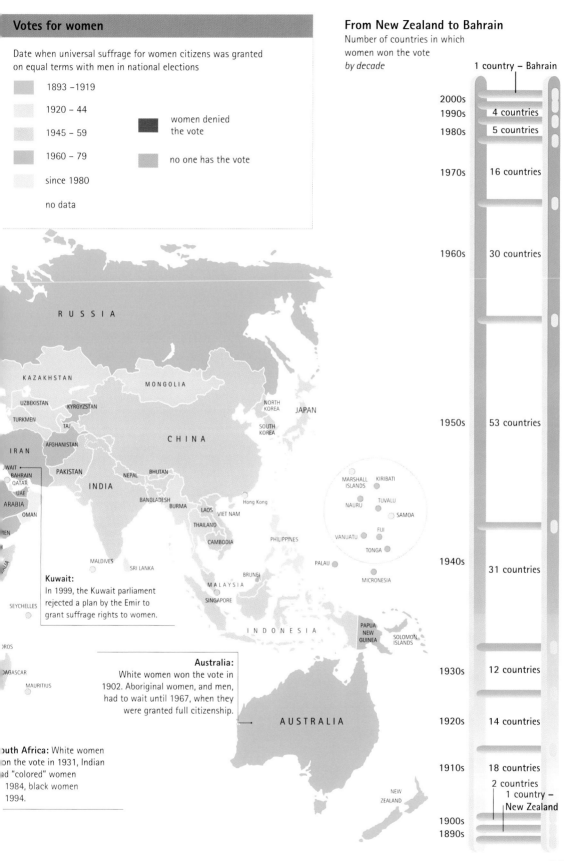

Votes for women

Date when universal suffrage for women citizens was granted on equal terms with men in national elections

- 1893 –1919
- 1920 – 44
- 1945 – 59
- 1960 – 79
- since 1980
- no data

- women denied the vote
- no one has the vote

Kuwait:
In 1999, the Kuwait parliament rejected a plan by the Emir to grant suffrage rights to women.

Australia:
White women won the vote in 1902. Aboriginal women, and men, had to wait until 1967, when they were granted full citizenship.

South Africa: White women won the vote in 1931, Indian and "colored" women 1984, black women 1994.

From New Zealand to Bahrain

Number of countries in which women won the vote
by decade

1 country – Bahrain

Decade	Countries
2000s	
1990s	4 countries
1980s	5 countries
1970s	16 countries
1960s	30 countries
1950s	53 countries
1940s	31 countries
1930s	12 countries
1920s	14 countries
1910s	18 countries
1900s	2 countries / 1 country – New Zealand
1890s	

93

This map is a snapshot of women's representation in government in early 2002. A few patterns persist across time and place: nowhere do women have equal representation with men in government; in only 22 countries do women represent 25 percent or more of elected legislators; the states with the highest shares of women in elected office are those that enforce explicit policies promoting equality – most notably, countries in Scandinavia.

The world average of women in legislatures dropped dramatically between the mid-1980s and the mid-1990s, the result of sweeping political changes in Eastern Europe and the former USSR, which resulted in a sharp drop in women's representation in government in those states.

The presence of women in government is important not only for the rights of women, but, perhaps, for the nature of governance itself. Recent studies suggest that when women are elected in sufficient numbers they introduce different perceptions of the norms of appropriate governance. In only a few states have women achieved a "critical mass" of elected representation.

In many countries, elected officials have little influence over actual governance. Authoritarian regimes abound, and other states have weak legislatures. Nonetheless, electing women even to weak legislatures can have considerable symbolic significance – as is demonstrated by the change in governance in Afghanistan between 2001 and 2002.

Ministerial positions
Percentage of ministerial positions held by women where over 25%
most recent since 1999

Sweden 55%
Denmark 43%
New Zealand 44%
Norway 42%
Finland 39%
Germany 39%
South Africa 38%
Zimbabwe 36%
Netherlands 36%
Hungary 36%

Honduras 33%
Mali 33%
Iceland 33%
UK 33%
USA 32%
Austria 31%
Gambia 31%
France 30%

Japan 29%
Switzerland 29%
Luxembourg 29%
Venezuela 29%
Costa Rica 29%
Botswana 27%
Uganda 27%
Belarus 26%
Chile 26%

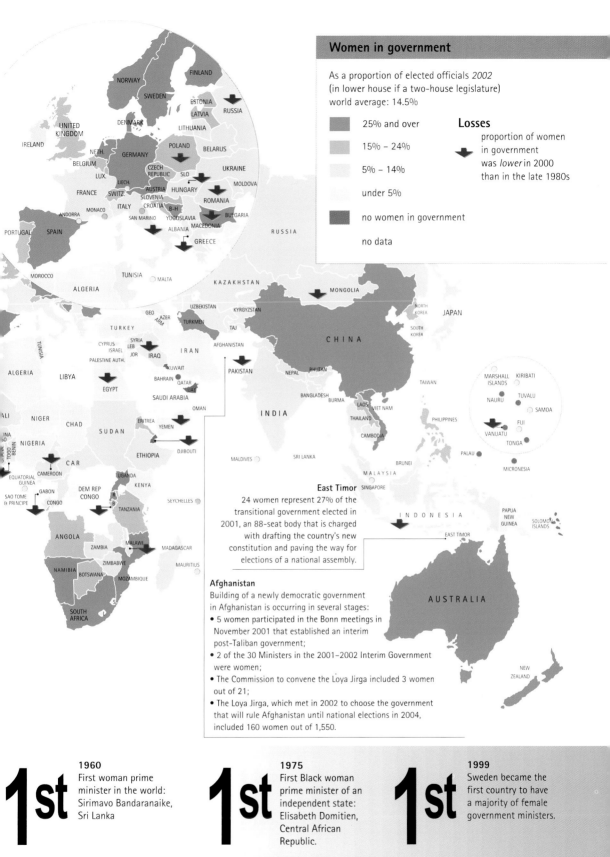

Women in government

As a proportion of elected officials *2002*
(in lower house if a two-house legislature)
world average: 14.5%

- 25% and over
- 15% – 24%
- 5% – 14%
- under 5%
- no women in government
- no data

Losses
proportion of women
in government
was *lower* in 2000
than in the late 1980s

East Timor
24 women represent 27% of the
transitional government elected in
2001, an 88-seat body that is charged
with drafting the country's new
constitution and paving the way for
elections of a national assembly.

Afghanistan
Building of a newly democratic government
in Afghanistan is occurring in several stages:
- 5 women participated in the Bonn meetings in
  November 2001 that established an interim
  post-Taliban government;
- 2 of the 30 Ministers in the 2001–2002 Interim Government
  were women;
- The Commission to convene the Loya Jirga included 3 women
  out of 21;
- The Loya Jirga, which met in 2002 to choose the government
  that will rule Afghanistan until national elections in 2004,
  included 160 women out of 1,550.

1st 1960
First woman prime
minister in the world:
Sirimavo Bandaranaike,
Sri Lanka

1st 1975
First Black woman
prime minister of an
independent state:
Elisabeth Domitien,
Central African
Republic.

1st 1999
Sweden became the
first country to have
a majority of female
government ministers.

Almost everywhere in the world women are now at least visible in national legislatures. An increasing number of countries and political parties have passed legislation to ensure this. Quota or reservation systems are now in place in more than 25 countries, although they are controversial, perhaps no more so than among women themselves.

Around the world, increasing numbers of women are active in local governance, in city councils and in mayoralties.

The ranks of heads of national government, though, remain resolutely male dominated. Only 35 countries have ever had a woman head of government, and some of those were in short-term caretaker positions. Women who hold ceremonial or non-elected "heads of state" positions are not included on the map, but women currently hold this office in Denmark, Iceland, the Netherlands, and the United Kingdom.

European Parliament
Percentage of women elected to
national delegations
to the Parliament of the European Union
2002

Total percentage of women in European Parliament 31%

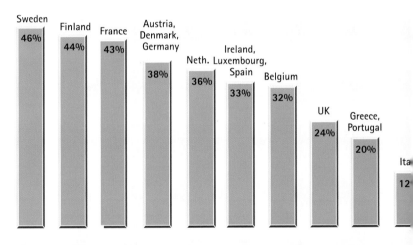

Sweden 46%
Finland 44%
France 43%
Austria, Denmark, Germany 38%
Neth. 36%
Ireland, Luxembourg, Spain 33%
Belgium 32%
UK 24%
Greece, Portugal 20%
Ita 12

Running the city
Women city and municipal mayors
2000 or latest available data
selected countries

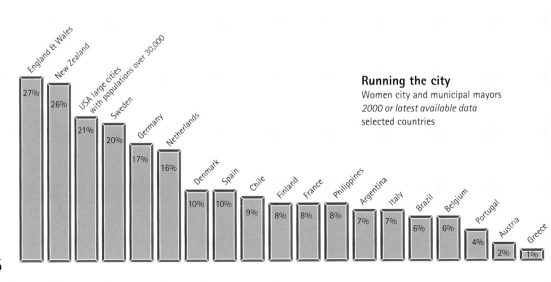

England & Wales 27%
New Zealand 26%
USA large cities with populations over 30,000 21%
Sweden 20%
Germany 17%
Netherlands 16%
Denmark 10%
Spain 10%
Chile 9%
Finland 8%
France 8%
Philippines 8%
Argentina 7%
Italy 7%
Brazil 6%
Belgium 6%
Portugal 4%
Austria 2%
Greece 1%

Candidate quotas

The 1995 "Platform for Action" from the UN Beijing conference called on governments to ensure "women's equal access to and full participation in power structures and decision making". Quotas are one route to this goal, although they are controversial and their success is mixed.

quotas in place *2001*

quota initiatives rejected *2001*

Finland: All government decision-making bodies must include a minimum of 40% women.

Latin America: Since 1991, twelve Latin American countries have adopted quota laws establishing a minimum level of 20%– 40% for women's participation as candidates in national elections – 1991: Argentina; 1996: Paraguay, Mexico; 1997: Bolivia, Brazil, Costa Rica, Ecuador, Panama, Peru, Dominican Republic; 1998: Venezuela; 1999: Colombia.

France: In 1999, a constitutional amendment was passed requiring political parties to put up 50% women candidates in almost all local and national elections; in 2001, this resulted in a leap from 22% to 48% women in local councils.

Austria, Germany, Italy, Mozambique, South Africa, Turkey, UK: One or more of the major political parties have adopted quotas for women candidates.

India: 33% of the seats on village and district councils are reserved for women; by 2001, there were close to 1 million elected women leaders at the village level.

Bosnia-Herzegovina: The percentage of women in the House of Representatives jumped from 2% in 1996 to 26% in 1998, after regulations were introduced requiring parties to put forward at least 30% women candidates.

Uganda: The 1995 constitution stipulated that a minimum of one-third of all seats in local councils must be filled by women.

South Africa: The African National Congress party enacted a 30% quota for female candidates in 1994.

Tanzania: 20% of national seats and 25% of local government seats are reserved for women.

LATVIA
POLAND
SWITZERLAND
REP MOLDOVA
EAST TIMOR

Heads of government

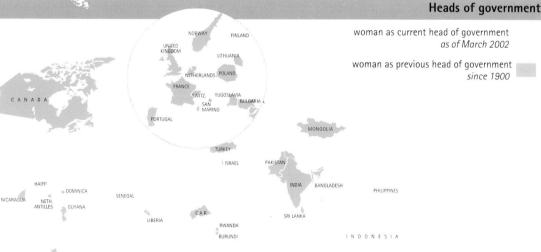

woman as current head of government *as of March 2002*

woman as previous head of government *since 1900*

CANADA
NORWAY
FINLAND
UNITED KINGDOM
LITHUANIA
NETHERLANDS
POLAND
FRANCE
SWITZ.
YUGOSLAVIA
SAN MARINO
BULGARIA
PORTUGAL
MONGOLIA
TURKEY
ISRAEL
PAKISTAN
HAITI
DOMINICA
SENEGAL
INDIA
BANGLADESH
PHILIPPINES
NICARAGUA
NETH. ANTILLES
GUYANA
LIBERIA
C A R
SRI LANKA
RWANDA
BURUNDI
INDONESIA
BOLIVIA
ARGENTINA
NEW ZEALAND

Many regions of the world are in extreme crisis, fractured by wars, insurgencies, ethnic conflicts, famine and economic collapse. Millions of people are displaced, and struggling for survival against great odds. The global population of refugees, including internally displaced people, is estimated at between 35 and 45 million. Most armed conflicts today are civil wars, and most of these involve the deliberate targeting of civilians.

Women bear specific burdens in crisis zones. Their responsibility for sustaining families is increased, but the resources available to meet those needs are diminished. Prostitution and the trafficking of girls and women (see Map 20) increases as a result of armed insurgent strategy or civilian destitution. Wartime rape is endemic and often systematic.

Sexual offences as acts of war have been broadly proscribed since the1940s, but it was only in the mid-1990s that feminists succeeded in having war rape specifically designated as a prosecutable war crime.

Gender imbalance

Women and men in major host-country populations of refugees, asylum-seekers, and internally displaced people *2001*

Worldwide, women constitute 50% – 55% of refugees, but men often have greater opportunities for seeking asylum.

More women than men
Croatia
Georgia
Burundi
Djibouti

More men than women
Belarus, Colombia, Iran, South Africa, Uzbekistan, Austria, Central African Republic, Kenya, Malaysia, Saudi Arabia, Sri Lanka, France, Mauritania, Somalia

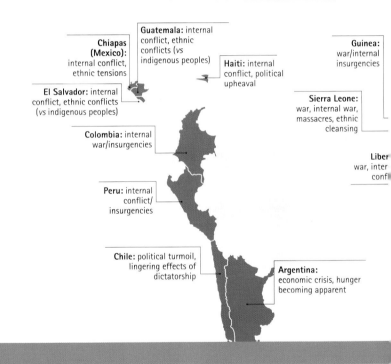

Chiapas (Mexico): internal conflict, ethnic tensions

Guatemala: internal conflict, ethnic conflicts (*vs* indigenous peoples)

Haiti: internal conflict, political upheaval

Guinea: war/internal insurgencies

El Salvador: internal conflict, ethnic conflicts (*vs* indigenous peoples)

Sierra Leone: war, internal war, massacres, ethnic cleansing

Colombia: internal war/insurgencies

Liber war, inter confl

Peru: internal conflict/ insurgencies

Chile: political turmoil, lingering effects of dictatorship

Argentina: economic crisis, hunger becoming apparent

Refugees

Countries of origin of largest populations of refugees *2001*

Host countries to largest populations of refugees *2001*

Countries with largest populations of internally displaced people *2001*

Afghanistan **approx 4.5 million**
Palestinians **approx 4.1 million**
Burundi **568,000**
Iraq **513,000**
Sudan **490,000**

Iran **2.5 million**
Pakistan **2 million**
Jordan **1.6 million**
Gaza **853,000**
West Bank **608,000**

Sudan **4 million**
Colombia **2.4 million**
Angola **2–3 million**
DR Congo **2 million**
Indonesia **1.4 million**

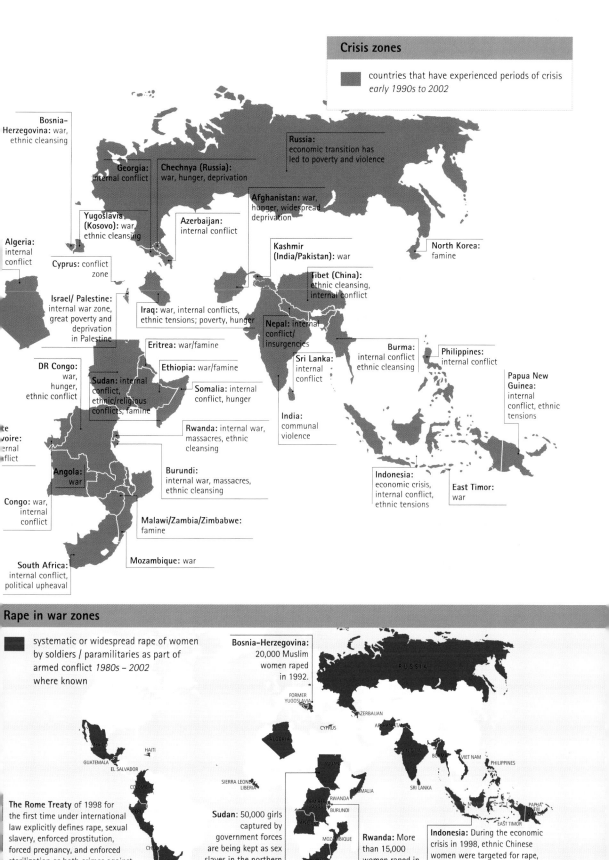

Crisis zones

■ countries that have experienced periods of crisis *early 1990s to 2002*

Bosnia–Herzegovina: war, ethnic cleansing

Russia: economic transition has led to poverty and violence

Georgia: internal conflict

Chechnya (Russia): war, hunger, deprivation

Afghanistan: war, hunger, widespread deprivation

Yugoslavia (Kosovo): war, ethnic cleansing

Azerbaijan: internal conflict

North Korea: famine

Algeria: internal conflict

Kashmir (India/Pakistan): war

Cyprus: conflict zone

Tibet (China): ethnic cleansing, internal conflict

Israel/ Palestine: internal war zone, great poverty and deprivation in Palestine

Iraq: war, internal conflicts, ethnic tensions; poverty, hunger

Nepal: internal conflict/ insurgencies

Burma: internal conflict ethnic cleansing

Philippines: internal conflict

Eritrea: war/famine

Sri Lanka: internal conflict

Papua New Guinea: internal conflict, ethnic tensions

DR Congo: war, hunger, ethnic conflict

Ethiopia: war/famine

Sudan: internal conflict, ethnic/religious conflicts, famine

Somalia: internal conflict, hunger

India: communal violence

Rwanda: internal war, massacres, ethnic cleansing

te voire: ernal flict

Angola: war

Burundi: internal war, massacres, ethnic cleansing

Indonesia: economic crisis, internal conflict, ethnic tensions

East Timor: war

Congo: war, internal conflict

Malawi/Zambia/Zimbabwe: famine

South Africa: internal conflict, political upheaval

Mozambique: war

Rape in war zones

■ systematic or widespread rape of women by soldiers / paramilitaries as part of armed conflict *1980s – 2002* where known

Bosnia–Herzegovina: 20,000 Muslim women raped in 1992.

The Rome Treaty of 1998 for the first time under international law explicitly defines rape, sexual slavery, enforced prostitution, forced pregnancy, and enforced sterilization as both crimes against humanity and war crimes.

Sudan: 50,000 girls captured by government forces are being kept as sex slaves in the northern territories.

Rwanda: More than 15,000 women raped in 1994 genocide.

Indonesia: During the economic crisis in 1998, ethnic Chinese women were targeted for rape, including gang rapes reported by 168 women.

99

Military service is traditionally the preserve of men – and they have fought hard to keep it that way. Contested constructions of femininity and masculinity shape the debates about whether women should participate in militaries. Militaries have been imagined as proving grounds for masculinity; allowing women in challenges ideals of both male and female behaviour. Military strategists also argue that the presence of women interferes with the male bonding essential to military "readiness." Similar arguments have been raised against gays and lesbians serving in militaries.

Among feminists, too, women's participation in militaries is controversial. On the one hand, militaries provide employment opportunities, and military service is represented as the pinnacle of service to the nation. On the other hand, it is argued that women's participation in masculinized institutions of organized violence harms the long-term interests of all women.

Restrictions on women's participation

2001 where known

● restrictions exist
women excluded from holding certain military posts

○ no restrictions
women can serve in all military positions

Firts

USA 1993
US lifts the Air Force ban
on women flying combat missions

UK 1995, Taiwan 1996
First women pilots
certified to fly combat airplanes.

Israel 1995
Supreme Court rules
women must be allowed
to train as combat pilots.

Norway 1995
World's first wom
submarine commar

Brazil 1995, Argentina 1996
Austria 1998, Italy 2000
Women allowed to serve
in active duty forces
for the first time.

Out in the forces

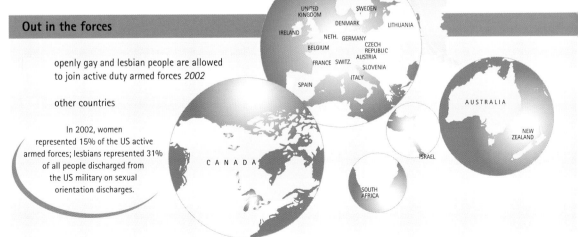

openly gay and lesbian people are allowed
to join active duty armed forces *2002*

other countries

In 2002, women
represented 15% of the US active
armed forces; lesbians represented 31%
of all people discharged from
the US military on sexual
orientation discharges.

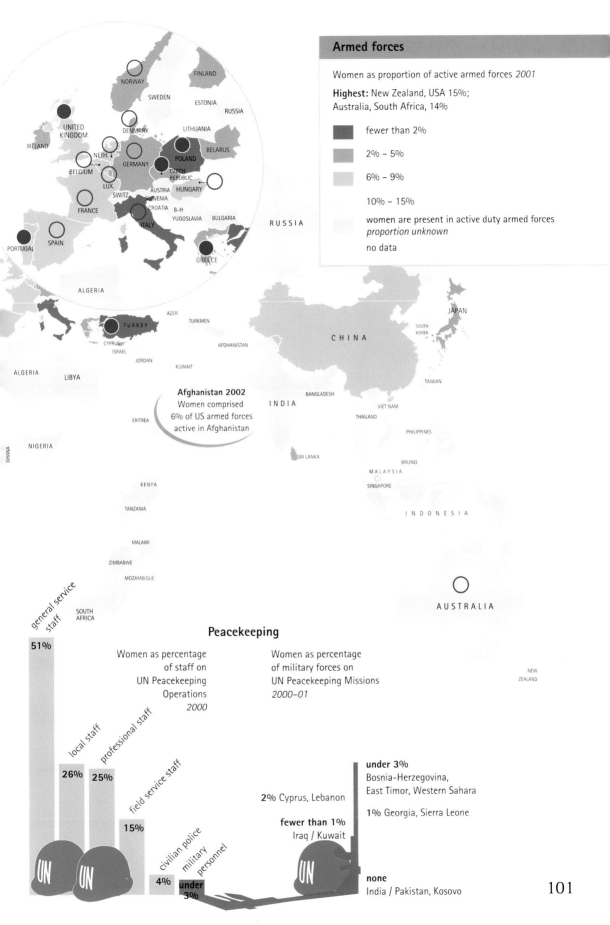

Armed forces

Women as proportion of active armed forces *2001*

Highest: New Zealand, USA 15%;
Australia, South Africa, 14%

- fewer than 2%
- 2% – 5%
- 6% – 9%
- 10% – 15%
- women are present in active duty armed forces *proportion unknown*
- no data

Afghanistan 2002
Women comprised
6% of US armed forces
active in Afghanistan

Peacekeeping

Women as percentage
of staff on
UN Peacekeeping
Operations
2000

- general service staff **51%**
- local staff **26%**
- professional staff **25%**
- field service staff **15%**
- civilian police **4%**
- military personnel **under 3%**

Women as percentage
of military forces on
UN Peacekeeping Missions
2000–01

2% Cyprus, Lebanon

fewer than 1%
Iraq / Kuwait

under 3%
Bosnia-Herzegovina,
East Timor, Western Sahara

1% Georgia, Sierra Leone

none
India / Pakistan, Kosovo

101

Feminist Organizing

Norway 2002
Government orders companies to ensure that at least 40% of their board members are women. State-owned firms have just 12 months to comply, the 650 public companies have up to 3 years. If they fail to meet the deadlines, the government will bring in legislation to enforce the quotas.

Netherlands 2001
Gay and lesbian marriages granted full recognition on equal terms with heterosexual marriages.

USA
2000 Government approves use of RU486, a non-surgical abortifacent.
1996 Government directive officially prohibits US military personnel from engaging in child prostitution. The directive states that "any use of child prostitutes is an egregious exploitation of children...and... is detrimental to the health and welfare of service members and the ability of the US forces to carry out their mission."

Scotland 2002
Members of Scottish Episcopal Church in Edinburgh vote in favor of law allowing women to become bishops.

UK 2001
The "morning-after" contraceptive pill becomes available without a prescription for women over the age of 16.

Austria 199
The Vienr Philharmon agrees to adm women as player it had been an a male institutic since its foundir in 184

France 1999
Constitutional amendment requires political parties to put up 50% women candidates in elections.

Germany 2001
Women gain right to enter all divisions of the German military; previously, women were only allowed to serve the military in medical staff positions and musical units.

Colombia
2002 About 20,000 women participate in a women's peace march in Bogota to demand the end to the civil war, many shouting "We won't give birth to more sons to send to war."
2001 The Mayor of Bogota calls for a one-night curfew on all men, forbidding them to be out in the city streets for a night in order to draw attention to epidemic rates of violence against women.

Senegal 1999
Senegalese women win national ban on female circumcision.

"Never doubt that a small group of thoughtful committed citizens can change the world; indeed, it's the only thing that ever has."
— Margaret Mead

"It is not acceptable for women to constitute 70 percent of the world's 1.3 billion absolute poor. Nor is it acceptable for women to work two-thirds of the world's working hours, but earn only one-tenth of the world's income and own less than one-tenth of the world's property. Many fundamental changes must be made."
— Noleen Heyzer
UNIFEM Director
Plenary Address to the Fourth
World Conference on Women

Brazil 2001
Brazil legislature passes sweeping changes to the Civil Code granting equal rights to women in marriage and divorce, in household decision-making authority, and in a wide range of family matters.

Chad 2002
Parliament passes a law guaranteeing protection for reproductive health rights. The new law makes it an offence to engage in any form of sexual violence, including female genital cutting, forced marriage, domestic violence or sexual slavery. Chadians living with HIV/AIDS are also guaranteed basic health care and confidentiality, according to the provisions of the law. It also codifies the right of Chadians to decide freely when and whom to marry, and guarantees them the right to information about family planning methods.

Peru 1997
Repeal of 1924 law allowing men who rape women to escape punishment by marrying their victims. The law also allowed men involved in a gang rape to go free if one of the men married the woman.

South Africa 1994
New constitution grants equal rights between men and women, and equal rights for gays and lesbians.

Botswana 199
First woman appointed serve as a High Cou Justic

1996 International War Crimes Court, The Hague: a United Nations' tribunal indicts eight Bosnian Serb military and police officers in connection with rapes of Muslim women in the Bosnian war, marking the first time sexual assault has been treated separately as a crime of war.

2000 The UN Security Council passes Resolution 1325, mandating the equal participation of women in peacekeeping and post-conflict reconstruction.

2001 Irene Zubaida Khan becomes the first woman Secretary-General of Amnesty International.

Iran 2002
Parliament approves a bill granting women the right to seek a divorce in court – a right women have not had since the 1979 Islamic Revolution. The Guardian Council is likely to block passage of the bill into law, but parliamentary approval sets an important precedent.

Lithuania 2002
The government repeals a requirement that women undergo a gynecological exam to qualify for a driver's license. The law was based on a medical assumption that certain "women's diseases" could cause sufficient pain to inhibit driving.

Afghanistan 2002
First women's reproductive health center opens in Kabul.

China 1996
First battered women's shelter opens.

Jordan 2002
New marital law allows women to initiate divorces.

Palestinian Territories 1995
Birzeit University establishes the first Women's Studies program at a Palestinian university.

Pakistan 2001
A women-only post office opens in Karachi.

Bahrain 2002
Women allowed to vote and run for all elected offices.

Nepal 2002
Reversing 150 years of legal discrimination against women, Nepal's Parliament passed an amendment to the Civil Code that partially legalizes abortion and that institutes sweeping changes in many other discriminatory laws, including inheritance rights, marriage and divorce laws, and laws against sexual violence.

Vietnam 2002
Government bans polygamy and dowries in marriage.

Rwanda 2000
New law gives women the right to inherit property on equal terms with men.

Malaysia 2000
Women lawyers allowed to wear trousers in court.

Turkey 2001
Turkish parliament adopts a revision to the country's Civil Code formally recognizing women's equality. Under the revised code, women no longer need their husband's permission to work outside the home. Married women will now enjoy property rights and will be able to keep their maiden names if they choose. Women will also be able to sue for divorce if their husbands commit adultery and will be entitled to alimony and compensation. The Flying Broom, a Turkish women's rights group, hailed the new code as an "historic turning point."

Australia 2002
The Australian Capital Territory becomes the first state or territory in Australia to completely remove abortion from the criminal code.

Demography and Health

Countries	1 Population 2001		2 Households Average number of people per household mid-1990s or latest available data	3 Marriage % of women aged 15–19 who are married 1999 or latest available data	4 Motherhood Average number of childbirths per woma 2000 or latest available data
	total thousands	women as % of total			
Afghanistan	22,474	48%	–	54%	6.9
Albania	3,145	49%	4.3	8%	2.5
Algeria	30,841	49%	7	10%	3.8
Angola	13,528	51%	–	36%	6.8
Argentina	37,487	51%	3.7	12%	2.6
Armenia	3,788	52%	4.4	23%	1.7
Australia	19,339	50%	3	2%	1.8
Austria	8,075	51%	2.5	3%	1.4
Azerbaijan	8,097	51%	4.5	12%	2
Bahamas	308	51%	4.1	4%	2.6
Bahrain	651	43%	5.6	7%	2.9
Bangladesh	140,369	48%	5.5	51%	3.1
Belarus	10,148	53%	2.7	11%	1.4
Belgium	10,263	51%	2.4	2%	1.6
Belize	231	49%	4.8	2%	3.7
Benin	6,446	51%	5.9	30%	5.8
Bhutan	2,141	49%	–	–	5.5
Bolivia	8,517	50%	3.6	14%	4.4
Bosnia-Herzegovina	4,067	51%	–	–	1.4
Botswana	1,554	51%	4.8	6%	4.4
Brazil	172,559	51%	4.2	17%	2.3
Brunei	335	47%	5.6	8%	2.8
Bulgaria	7,866	51%	2.8	17%	1.2
Burkina Faso	11,856	52%	6.2	35%	6.6
Burma	48,363	50%	–	7%	2.4
Burundi	6,502	51%	4.6	9%	6.3
Cambodia	13,440	51%	–	–	4.6
Cameroon	15,203	50%	5.2	36%	5.3
Canada	31,015	50%	2.6	1%	1.6
Central African Rep.	3,782	51%	4.7	42%	4.9
Chad	8,135	51%	–	49%	6.1
Chile	15,401	50%	4	12%	2.4
China	1,284,971	49%	4	5%	1.8
Colombia	42,803	51%	4.3	20%	2.8
Comoros	727	50%	6.2	12%	4.8
Congo	3,111	51%	–	56%	6.1
Congo, Dem. Rep.	52,522	50%	–	74%	6.4
Costa Rica	4,113	49%	–	16%	2.8
Côte d'Ivoire	16,348	49%	6	28%	5.1
Croatia	4,655	52%	3.1	5%	1.6
Cuba	11,237	50%	4	29%	1.6
Cyprus	791	50%	3.2	8%	2

Sources: UN. The World's Women 2000 (**Cols 1, 2 3, 4**); Economic Commission for Europe. *Women & Men in Europe & North America.* 2000 (**Col 2**); UNICEF. *Early Marriage/ Child Spouses.* Innocenti Digest #7, March 2001 (**Col 3**); UN Dept of Economic & Social Affairs. *World Marriage Patterns 200* (**Col 3**);

5 Maternal Mortality Deaths of mothers per 100,000 live births mid-1990s or latest available data	6 Contraception % of married women using "modern" contraception 2001 or latest available data	7 HIV / AIDS 2001			Countries
		Number living with HIV / AIDS	% of pop. with HIV / AIDS	AIDS deaths in 2001	
820	2%	–	–	–	Afghanistan
31	–	–	–	–	Albania
150	49%	–	–	–	Algeria
1,300	–	350,000	5.50%	24,000	Angola
85	–	130,000	0.70%	1,800	Argentina
29	22%	2,400	0.20%	<100	Armenia
6	63%	12,000	0.10%	<100	Australia
11	53%	9,900	0.20%	<100	Austria
37	–	1,400	<0.1%	<100	Azerbaijan
10	–	6,200	3.50%	610	Bahamas
38	31%	<1,000	0.30%	–	Bahrain
600	43%	13,000	<0.1%	650	Bangladesh
33	42%	15,000	0.30%	1,000	Belarus
8	74%	8,500	0.20%	<100	Belgium
140	44%	2,500	2.00%	300	Belize
880	3%	120,000	3.60%	8,100	Benin
500	8%	<100	<0.1%	–	Bhutan
550	25%	4,600	0.10%	290	Bolivia
15	–	–	–	–	Bosnia-Herzegovina
480	41%	330,000	38.80%	26,000	Botswana
260	70%	610,000	0.70%	8,400	Brazil
22	–	–	–	–	Brunei
23	46%	–	–	–	Bulgaria
1,400	5%	440,000	6.50%	44,000	Burkina Faso
170	28%	–	–	–	Burma
1,900	1%	390,000	8.30%	40,000	Burundi
590	19%	170,000	2.70%	12,000	Cambodia
720	7%	920,000	11.80%	53,000	Cameroon
6	66%	55,000	0.30%	<500	Canada
1,200	3%	250,000	12.90%	22,000	Central African Rep.
1,500	1%	150,000	3.60%	14,000	Chad
33	–	20,000	0.30%	220	Chile
60	81%	850,000	0.10%	30,100	China
120	63%	140,000	0.40%	5,600	Colombia
570	11%	–	–	–	Comoros
1,100	–	110,000	7.20%	11,000	Congo
940	3%	1,300,000	4.90%	120,000	Congo, Dem. Rep.
35	72%	11,000	0.60%	890	Costa Rica
1,200	7%	770,000	9.70%	75,000	Côte d'Ivoire
18	–	200	<0.1%	<10	Croatia
24	67%	3,200	<0.1%	120	Cuba
–	–	<1,000	0.30%	–	Cyprus

DP. *Human Development Report 2001* (**Cols 4, 5**); UNICEF. *State of the World's Children*, 2002 (**Col 5**); UNFPA. *The State of World Population 2001* ols 5, 6); Population Reference Bureau. *2001 World Population Data Sheet* (**Col 6**); UNAIDS (**Col 7**)

Demography and Health

Countries	1 Population 2001		2 Households Average number of people per household mid-1990s or latest available data	3 Marriage % of women aged 15–19 who are married 1999 or latest available data	4 Motherhood Average number of childbirths per woman 2000 or latest available data
	total thousands	women as % of total			
Czech Republic	10,260	51%	2.5	4%	1.2
Denmark	5,332	50%	2.2	5%	1.7
Djibouti	643	53%	6.6	7%	5.3
Dominican Republic	8,507	49%	4.5	22%	2.8
Ecuador	12,880	50%	4.8	20%	3.1
Egypt	69,080	49%	4.9	16%	3.4
El Salvador	6,400	51%	4.1	16%	3.2
Equatorial Guinea	470	51%	–	26%	5.6
Eritrea	3,815	50%	–	38%	5.7
Estonia	1,377	53%	2.3	10%	1.3
Ethiopia	64,460	50%	–	31%	6.3
Fiji	822	49%	5.7	13%	2.7
Finland	5,178	51%	2.2	1%	1.7
France	59,453	51%	2.5	1%	1.7
Gabon	1,262	50%	–	16%	5.4
Gambia	1,337	51%	–	44%	5.2
Georgia	5,238	52%	3.6	19%	1.9
Germany	82,008	51%	2.2	1%	1.3
Ghana	19,734	50%	4.8	22%	5.2
Greece	10,624	51%	3	6%	1.3
Guatemala	11,687	50%	–	24%	4.9
Guinea	8,274	50%	7.2	49%	5.5
Guinea-Bissau	1,227	51%	7.9	–	5.8
Guyana	763	52%	–	7%	2.3
Haiti	8,270	51%	5	17%	4.4
Honduras	6,574	50%	5.4	30%	4.3
Hungary	9,917	52%	2.6	5%	1.4
Iceland	281	50%	2.7	1%	2.1
India	1,025,096	48%	5.5	36%	3.1
Indonesia	214,840	50%	4.5	18%	2.6
Iran	71,369	49%	5.1	26%	2.8
Iraq	23,585	49%	7.3	28%	5.3
Ireland	3,841	50%	3.1	1%	1.9
Israel	6,173	51%	3.5	5%	2.7
Italy	57,503	52%	2.7	3%	1.2
Jamaica	2,598	51%	–	1%	2.5
Japan	127,334	51%	3	1%	1.4
Jordan	5,051	48%	6.9	9%	4.9
Kazakhstan	16,095	52%	3.6	12%	2.3
Kenya	31,293	50%	5.2	17%	4.5
Korea (North)	22,428	50%	–	–	1.7
Korea (South)	47,069	50%	3.7	1%	2.1

Sources: UN. The World's Women 2000 (**Cols 1, 2 3, 4**); Economic Commission for Europe. *Women & Men in Europe & North America.* 2000 (**Col 2**); UNICEF. *Early Marriage/ Child Spouses.* Innocenti Digest #7, March 2001 (**Col 3**); UN Dept of Economic & Social Affairs. *World Marriage Patterns 200* (**Col 3**);

5 Maternal Mortality Deaths of mothers per 100,000 live births mid-1990s or latest available data	6 Contraception % of married women using "modern" contraception 2001 or latest available data	7 HIV / AIDS 2001			Countries
		Number living with HIV / AIDS	% of pop. with HIV / AIDS	AIDS deaths in 2001	
14	45%	500	<0.1%	<10	Czech Republic
15	72%	3,800	0.20%	<100	Denmark
520	–	–	–	–	Djibouti
110	59%	130,000	2.50%	7,800	Dominican Republic
210	52%	20,000	0.30%	1,700	Ecuador
170	54%	8,000	<0.1%	–	Egypt
180	54%	24,000	0.60%	2,100	El Salvador
1,400	–	5,900	3.40%	370	Equatorial Guinea
1,100	4%	55,000	2.80%	350	Eritrea
80	56%	7,700	1.00%	<100	Estonia
1,800	6%	2,100,000	6.40%	160,000	Ethiopia
20	35%	300	0.10%	–	Fiji
6	75%	1,200	<0.1%	<100	Finland
20	69%	100,000	0.30%	800	France
620	12%	–	–	–	Gabon
1,100	7%	8,400	1.60%	400	Gambia
22	20%	900	<0.1%	<100	Georgia
12	79%	41,000	0.10%	660	Germany
590	13%	360,000	3.00%	28,000	Ghana
2	–	8,800	0.20%	<100	Greece
270	31%	67,000	1.00%	5,200	Guatemala
1,200	4%	–	–	–	Guinea
910	–	17,000	2.80%	1,200	Guinea-Bissau
150	28%	18,000	2.70%	1,300	Guyana
1,100	22%	250,000	6.10%	30,000	Haiti
220	41%	57,000	1.60%	3,300	Honduras
23	68%	2,800	0.10%	<100	Hungary
16	–	220	0.20%	<100	Iceland
440	43%	3,970,000	0.80%	–	India
470	55%	120,000	0.10%	4,600	Indonesia
130	55%	20,000	<0.1%	290	Iran
370	10%	<1,000	<0.1%	–	Iraq
9	–	2,400	0.10%	<100	Ireland
8	–	–	–	–	Israel
11	56%	100,000	0.40%	1,100	Italy
120	63%	20,000	1.20%	980	Jamaica
12	53%	12,000	<0.1%	430	Japan
41	39%	<1,000	<0.1%	–	Jordan
80	53%	6,000	0.10%	300	Kazakhstan
1,300	32%	2,500,000	15.00%	190,000	Kenya
35	53%	–	–	–	Korea (North)
20	66%	4,000	<0.1%	220	Korea (South)

DP. *Human Development Report 2001* (**Cols 4, 5**); UNICEF. *State of the World's Children,* 2002 (**Col 5**); UNFPA. *The State of World Population 2001* ols **5, 6**); Population Reference Bureau. *2001 World Population Data Sheet* (**Col 6**); UNAIDS (**Col 7**)

Demography and Health

Countries	1 Population 2001		2 Households Average number of people per household mid-1990s or latest available data	3 Marriage % of women aged 15–19 who are married 1999 or latest available data	4 Motherhood Average number of childbirths per woman 2000 or latest available data
	total thousands	women as % of total			
Kuwait	1,971	42%	6.5	13%	2.9
Kyrgyzstan	4,986	51%	4.5	15%	3.2
Laos	5,403	50%	–	20%	5.8
Latvia	2,406	54%	3.1	11%	1.3
Lebanon	3,556	51%	–	13%	2.7
Lesotho	2,057	50%	5.1	18%	4.8
Liberia	3,108	50%	5	36%	6.3
Libya	5,408	48%	–	1%	3.8
Lithuania	3,689	53%	3.2	9%	1.4
Luxembourg	443	51%	2.6	2%	1.7
Macedonia	2,044	50%	3.9	9%	2.1
Madagascar	16,437	50%	4.5	34%	5.4
Malawi	11,572	50%	4.3	44%	6.8
Malaysia	22,633	49%	4.8	8%	3.2
Maldives	300	49%	6.8	37%	5.4
Mali	11,678	50%	5.6	50%	6.6
Mauritania	2,747	50%	–	36%	5.5
Mauritius	1,171	50%	4.4	12%	1.9
Mexico	100,368	51%	5	16%	2.8
Moldova	4,285	52%	3.4	15%	1.8
Mongolia	2,559	50%	–	–	2.6
Morocco	30,430	50%	6	11%	3.1
Mozambique	18,644	51%	–	47%	6.3
Namibia	1,788	51%	5.2	8%	4.9
Nepal	23,594	49%	5.6	42%	4.5
Netherlands	15,929	50%	2.3	2%	1.5
New Zealand	3,808	51%	2.8	1%	2
Nicaragua	5,208	50%	–	37%	4.4
Niger	11,227	50%	6.4	62%	6.8
Nigeria	116,929	50%	5.4	36%	5.2
Norway	4,488	50%	2.2	1%	1.9
Oman	2,623	47%	7	21%	5.9
Pakistan	144,971	49%	6.5	22%	5
Panama	2,899	50%	4.4	21%	2.6
Papua New Guinea	4,920	48%	–	21%	4.6
Paraguay	5,637	50%	4.7	17%	4.2
Peru	26,093	50%	5.2	13%	3
Philippines	77,131	50%	5.3	11%	3.6
Poland	38,577	51%	3.1	4%	1.5
Portugal	10,034	52%	3	6%	1.4
Qatar	575	35%	5.6	15%	3.7
Romania	22,388	51%	3.1	10%	1.2

Sources: UN. The World's Women 2000 (**Cols 1, 2 3, 4**); Economic Commission for Europe. *Women & Men in Europe & North America.* 2000 (**Col 2**); UNICEF. *Early Marriage/ Child Spouses.* Innocenti Digest #7, March 2001 (**Col 3**); UN Dept of Economic & Social Affairs. *World Marriage Patterns 200* (**Col 3**);

5 Maternal Mortality Deaths of mothers per 100,000 live births mid-1990s or latest available data	6 Contraception % of married women using "modern" contraception 2001 or latest available data	7 HIV / AIDS 2001			Countries
		Number living with HIV / AIDS	% of pop. with HIV / AIDS	AIDS deaths in 2001	
25	41%	–	–	–	Kuwait
80	49%	500	<0.1%	<100	Kyrgyzstan
650	21%	1,400	<0.1%	<150	Laos
70	51%	5,000	0.40%	<100	Latvia
130	37%	–	–	–	Lebanon
530	19%	360,000	31.00%	25,000	Lesotho
1,000	6%	–	–	–	Liberia
120	26%	7,000	0.20%	–	Libya
27	25%	1,300	0.10%	<100	Lithuania
–	–	–	0.20%	<100	Luxembourg
17	–	<100	<0.1%	<100	Macedonia
580	10%	22,000	0.30%	–	Madagascar
580	26%	850,000	15.00%	80,000	Malawi
39	30%	42,000	0.40%	2,500	Malaysia
390	–	<100	0.10%	–	Maldives
630	5%	110,000	1.70%	11,000	Mali
870	1%	–	–	–	Mauritania
45	60%	700	0.10%	<100	Mauritius
65	59%	150,000	0.30%	4,200	Mexico
65	50%	5,500	0.20%	300	Moldova
65	41%	<100	<0.1%	–	Mongolia
390	49%	13,000	0.10%	–	Morocco
980	5%	1,100,000	13.00%	60,000	Mozambique
370	26%	230,000	22.50%	13,000	Namibia
830	26%	58,000	0.50%	2,400	Nepal
10	71%	17,000	0.20%	110	Netherlands
15	72%	1,200	0.10%	<100	New Zealand
250	57%	5,800	0.20%	400	Nicaragua
920	5%	–	–	–	Niger
1,100	9%	3,500,000	5.80%	170,000	Nigeria
9	69%	1,800	0.10%	<100	Norway
120	18%	1,300	0.10%	–	Oman
200	13%	78,000	0.10%	4,500	Pakistan
100	54%	25,000	1.50%	1,900	Panama
390	20%	17,000	0.70%	880	Papua New Guinea
170	48%	–	–	–	Paraguay
240	50%	53,000	0.40%	3,900	Peru
240	32%	9,400	<0.1%	720	Philippines
12	12%	–	–	–	Poland
12	33%	27,000	0.50%	1,000	Portugal
41	32%	–	–	–	Qatar
60	30%	6,500	<0.1%	350	Romania

UNDP. *Human Development Report 2001* (**Cols 4, 5**); UNICEF. *State of the World's Children*, 2002 (**Col 5**); UNFPA. *The State of World Population 2001* (**Cols 5, 6**); Population Reference Bureau. *2001 World Population Data Sheet* (**Col 6**); UNAIDS (**Col 7**)

Demography and Health

Countries	1 Population 2001		2 Households Average number of people per household mid-1990s or latest available data	3 Marriage % of women aged 15–19 who are married 1999 or latest available data	4 Motherhood Average number of childbirths per woman 2000 or latest available data
	total thousands	women as % of total			
Russia	144,664	53%	2.8	14%	1.3
Rwanda	7,949	50%	4.7	10%	6.2
Samoa	159	47%	6.7	7%	4.2
Saudi Arabia	21,028	47%	7.4	16%	5.8
Senegal	9,662	50%	8.8	44%	5.6
Seychelles	0	–	4.5	6%	–
Sierra Leone	4,587	51%	5.7	6%	6.1
Singapore	4,108	50%	4.2	1%	1.7
Slovakia	5,404	51%	2.9	7%	1.4
Slovenia	1,986	51%	3.1	2%	1.3
Solomon Islands	463	49%	6.5	19%	4.9
Somalia	9,157	50%	–	–	7.3
South Africa	43,792	51%	5.8	5%	3.3
Spain	39,920	51%	3.2	2%	1.2
Sri Lanka	19,104	49%	–	7%	2.1
Sudan	31,809	50%	6.3	21%	4.6
Suriname	419	50%	–	–	2.2
Swaziland	938	51%	–	10%	4.7
Sweden	8,833	51%	2.1	1%	1.6
Switzerland	7,170	51%	2.3	10%	1.5
Syria	16,609	49%	6	25%	4
Tajikistan	6,135	50%	5.7	16%	4.2
Tanzania	35,965	50%	5.2	26%	5.5
Thailand	63,584	51%	4.4	15%	1.7
Togo	4,657	50%	5.1	20%	6.1
Trinidad & Tobago	1,300	50%	4.1	9%	1.7
Tunisia	9,562	50%	5.4	3%	2.6
Turkey	67,632	50%	4.4	16%	2.5
Turkmenistan	4,835	50%	5.2	7%	3.6
Uganda	24,022	50%	5.4	50%	7.1
Ukraine	49,111	54%	2.8	16%	1.4
United Arab Emirates	2,653	34%	–	18%	3.4
United Kingdom	59,541	51%	2.4	2%	1.7
United States of America	285,926	51%	2.6	4%	2
Uruguay	3,361	51%	3.3	11%	2.4
Uzbekistan	25,257	50%	5.1	15%	3.5
Venezuela	24,632	50%	4.8	18%	3
Vietnam	79,175	50%	4.8	11%	2.6
Yemen	19,114	50%	5.8	24%	7.6
Yugoslavia	10,538	50%	3.6	12%	1.8
Zambia	10,649	50%	5.6	27%	5.6
Zimbabwe	12,852	50%	5.2	21%	3.8

Sources: UN. The World's Women 2000 (**Cols 1, 2, 3, 4**); Economic Commission for Europe. *Women & Men in Europe & North America.* 2000 (**Col** UNICEF. *Early Marriage/ Child Spouses.* Innocenti Digest #7, March 2001 (**Col 3**); UN Dept of Economic & Social Affairs. *World Marriage Patterns 2* (**Col 3**);

5 Maternal Mortality Deaths of mothers per 100,000 live births mid-1990s or latest available data	6 Contraception % of married women using "modern" contraception 2001 or latest available data	7 HIV / AIDS 2001			Countries
		Number living with HIV / AIDS	% of pop. with HIV / AIDS	AIDS deaths in 2001	
75	49%	700,000	0.90%	9,000	Russia
2,300	4%	500,000	8.90%	49,000	Rwanda
15	–	–	–	–	Samoa
23	29%	–	–	–	Saudi Arabia
1,200	8%	27,000	0.50%	2,500	Senegal
–	–	–	–	–	Seychelles
2,100	–	170,000	7.00%	11,000	Sierra Leone
9	73%	3,400	0.20%	140	Singapore
14	41%	<100	<0.1%	<100	Slovakia
17	54%	280	<0.1%	<100	Slovenia
60	–	–	–	–	Solomon Islands
1,600	–	43,000	1.00%	–	Somalia
340	55%	5,000,000	20.10%	360,000	South Africa
8	71%	130,000	0.50%	2,300	Spain
60	44%	4,800	<0.1%	250	Sri Lanka
1,500	7%	450,000	2.60%	23,000	Sudan
230	–	3,700	1.20%	330	Suriname
370	19%	170,000	33.40%	12,000	Swaziland
8	72%	3,300	0.10%	<100	Sweden
8	78%	19,000	0.50%	<100	Switzerland
200	32%	–	–	–	Syria
120	–	200	<0.1%	<100	Tajikistan
1,100	17%	1,500,000	7.80%	140,000	Tanzania
44	70%	670,000	1.80%	55,000	Thailand
980	7%	150,000	6.00%	12,000	Togo
65	44%	17,000	2.50%	1,200	Trinidad & Tobago
70	49%	–	–	–	Tunisia
55	38%	–	–	–	Turkey
65	53%	<100	<0.1%	<100	Turkmenistan
1,100	8%	600,000	5.00%	84,000	Uganda
45	37%	250,000	1.00%	11,000	Ukraine
30	24%	–	–	–	United Arab Emirates
10	68%	34,000	0.10%	460	United Kingdom
12	71%	900,000	0.60%	15,000	United States of America
50	–	6,300	0.30%	<500	Uruguay
60	51%	740	<0.1%	<100	Uzbekistan
43	38%	–	–	–	Venezuela
95	56%	130,000	0.30%	6,600	Vietnam
850	10%	9,900	0.10%	–	Yemen
15	12%	10,000	0.20%	<100	Yugoslavia
870	14%	1,200,000	21.50%	120,000	Zambia
610	50%	2,300,000	33.70%	200,000	Zimbabwe

DP. *Human Development Report 2001* (**Cols 4, 5**); UNICEF. *State of the World's Children*, 2002 (**Col 5**); UNFPA. *The State of World Population 2001* ols 5, 6); Population Reference Bureau. *2001 World Population Data Sheet* (**Col 6**); UNAIDS (**Col 7**)

School, Work, Power

Countries	1 Gender Development Index country rank 2000	2 The Vote Date of women's suffrage on equal terms with men	3 Women Working % of women who are economically active 1999	4 Workplaces late 1990s % of economically active women working in:		
				agriculture	industry	services
Afghanistan	–	1965	–	–	–	–
Albania	74	1945	60%	–	–	–
Algeria	90	1962	29%	–	–	–
Angola	–	1975	73%	–	–	–
Argentina	33	1947	35%	<1%	12%	88%
Armenia	62	1921	62%	26%	19%	53%
Australia	1	1902	56%	4%	11%	85%
Austria	15	1918	45%	8%	14%	78%
Azerbaijan	–	1921	54%	–	–	–
Bahamas	38	1962	68%	1%	6%	93%
Bahrain	40	2001	32%	<0.1%	32%	67%
Bangladesh	121	1956	66%	78%	8%	11%
Belarus	50	1919	59%	12%	25%	60%
Belgium	2	1948	40%	2%	13%	86%
Belize	58	1954	27%	5%	–	–
Benin	134	1956	74%	–	–	–
Bhutan	–	1953	58%	–	–	–
Bolivia	96	1952	48%	2%	16%	82%
Bosnia-Herzegovina	–	1949	–	–	–	–
Botswana	104	1965	65%	–	–	–
Brazil	64	1932	44%	22%	9%	68%
Brunei	31	no one votes	49%	–	–	–
Bulgaria	53	1944	57%	–	–	–
Burkina Faso	143	1956	76%	–	–	–
Burma	106	1935	66%	–	–	–
Burundi	145	1961	83%	–	–	–
Cambodia	109	1956	82%	–	–	–
Cameroon	115	1956	49%	–	–	–
Canada	5	1918	60%	2%	12%	86%
Central African Rep.	139	1956	68%	–	–	–
Chad	140	1956	67%	–	–	–
Chile	39	1948	37%	4%	14%	81%
China	77	1949	73%	<0.1%	–	–
Colombia	56	1954	48%	–	21%	76%
Comoros	114	1956	62%	–	–	–
Congo	113	1956	59%	–	–	–
Congo, Dem. Rep.	131	1967	61%	–	–	–
Costa Rica	41	1949	37%	6%	17%	76%
Côte d'Ivoire	132	1952	44%	–	–	–
Croatia	43	1945	48%	18%	22%	60%
Cuba	–	1934	–	–	–	–
Cyprus	26	1960	49%	10%	18%	71%

Sources: UNDP. *Human Development Report 2002* (Cols 1, 3, 4, 5, 7 and 8); Inter-Parliamentary Union (Col 2); Economic Commission for Europe *Women and Men in Europe and North America*, 2000 (Cols 3 & 4) FAO. *GenderFacts*, 2002 (Col 4);

5 School enrolled in primary school 1999 or latest available data		6 University Women as a % of students 2000 or most recent available	7 Literacy 2000		8 Government Women as a % of elected officials 2002	Countries
girls	boys		% of women who are illiterate	% of men who are illiterate		
–	64%	–	80%	53%	–	Afghanistan
100%	100%	56%	23%	–	6%	Albania
100%	100%	44%	49%	26%	3%	Algeria
88%	95%	–	–	–	16%	Angola
100%	100%	–	3%	4%	31%	Argentina
91%	87%	56%	2%	1%	3%	Armenia
100%	100%	51%	1%	–	25%	Australia
100%	100%	49%	1%	–	27%	Austria
100%	100%	44%	–	–	11%	Azerbaijan
97%	97%	–	3%	1%	15%	Bahamas
100%	100%	57%	17%	11%	0%	Bahrain
66%	77%	20%	71%	51%	11%	Bangladesh
96%	100%	53%	1%	–	10%	Belarus
100%	100%	50%	1%	–	23%	Belgium
100%	100%	–	7%	–	7%	Belize
57%	98%	19%	76%	51%	6%	Benin
–	–	–	66%	44%	9%	Bhutan
90%	99%	–	21%	9%	12%	Bolivia
–	–	–	–	–	26%	Bosnia-Herzegovina
100%	100%	47%	20%	19%	17%	Botswana
100%	100%	53%	15%	17%	7%	Brazil
100%	100%	59%	12%	7%	–	Brunei
98%	100%	60%	2%	–	26%	Bulgaria
31%	48%	23%	87%	71%	8%	Burkina Faso
100%	100%	64%	19%	11%	–	Burma
46%	55%	26%	60%	51%	20%	Burundi
100%	100%	16%	42%	–	7%	Cambodia
84%	93%	–	31%	25%	6%	Cameroon
100%	100%	53%	1%	–	21%	Canada
45%	69%	9%	66%	32%	7%	Central African Rep.
39%	76%	12%	59%	38%	2%	Chad
100%	100%	46%	5%	5%	13%	Chile
100%	100%	36%	23%	10%	22%	China
100%	100%	52%	8%	9%	12%	Colombia
69%	84%	–	51%	36%	–	Comoros
100%	100%	19%	26%	17%	12%	Congo
59%	86%	–	51%	13%	–	Congo, Dem. Rep.
100%	100%	–	4%	5%	19%	Costa Rica
60%	82%	21%	62%	50%	9%	Côte d'Ivoire
87%	88%	51%	3%	–	21%	Croatia
100%	100%	60%	4%	4%	28%	Cuba
100%	100%	75%	5%	–	11%	Cyprus

The World's Women 2000: Trends and Statistics. NY, 2000 (**Cols 3, 4, 5 and 6**); UNESCO. *Statistical Yearbook 1999* (**Cols 5, 6 and 7**); UNIFEM.
Progress of the World's Women. 2000 Report (**Col 7**)

School, Work, Power

Countries	1 Gender Development Index country rank 2000	2 The Vote Date of women's suffrage on equal terms with men	3 Women Working % of women who are economically active 1999	4 Workplaces late 1990s % of economically active women working in:		
				agriculture	industry	services
Czech Republic	32	1920	62%	4%	29%	66%
Denmark	13	1915	62%	2%	15%	83%
Djibouti	–	1957	–	–	–	–
Dominican Republic	79	1942	40%	–	–	–
Ecuador	80	1929	32%	2%	16%	83%
Egypt	99	1956	35%	42%	9%	48%
El Salvador	87	1950	46%	7%	21%	72%
Equatorial Guinea	93	1963	46%	–	–	–
Eritrea	133	1955	75%	–	–	–
Estonia	–	1918	62%	8%	27%	65%
Ethiopia	142	1955	57%	88%	2%	11%
Fiji	65	1963	35%	–	–	–
Finland	8	1906	57%	5%	14%	81%
France	12	1944	48%	3%	14%	83%
Gabon	–	1956	63%	–	–	–
Gambia	136	1960	70%	–	–	–
Georgia	–	1921	56%	–	–	–
Germany	16	1918	48%	3%	19%	79%
Ghana	108	1954	81%	–	–	–
Greece	25	1952	38%	23%	13%	63%
Guatemala	100	1946	35%	–	–	–
Guinea	–	1958	78%	–	–	–
Guinea-Bissau	141	1977	57%	–	–	–
Guyana	85	1966	41%	–	–	–
Haiti	122	1950	57%	–	–	–
Honduras	98	1955	40%	7%	27%	66%
Hungary	35	1945	49%	4%	26%	71%
Iceland	7	1915	68%	4%	15%	81%
India	105	1950	42%	–	–	–
Indonesia	91	1945	55%	42%	16%	42%
Iran	83	1963	28%	–	40%	38%
Iraq		1980	–	–	–	–
Ireland	17	1922	36%	3%	15%	82%
Israel	22	1948	48%	1%	14%	84%
Italy	20	1945	38%	7%	22%	72%
Jamaica	67	1944	69%	11%	12%	77%
Japan	11	1945	51%	6%	24%	69%
Jordan	84	1974	26%	–	–	–
Kazakhstan	70.3	1924	61%	–	–	–
Kenya	112	1963	75%	–	–	–
Korea (North)	–	1946	–	–	–	–
Korea (South)	29	1948	53%	13%	21%	66%

Sources: UNDP. *Human Development Report 2002* (**Cols 1, 3, 4, 5, 7 and 8**); Inter-Parliamentary Union (**Col 2**); Economic Commission for Europe. *Women and Men in Europe and North America*, 2000 (**Cols 3 & 4**) FAO. *GenderFacts*, 2002 (**Col 4**);

5 School		6 University	7 Literacy		8 Government	Countries
% enrolled in primary school 1999 or latest available data		Women as a % of students 2000 or most recent available	2000		Women as a % of elected officials 2002	
girls	boys		% of women who are illiterate	% of men who are illiterate		
100%	100%	48%	–	–	15%	Czech Republic
100%	100%	54%	1%	–	38%	Denmark
33%	44%	44%	62%	40%	0%	Djibouti
94%	94%	57%	16%	18%	16%	Dominican Republic
100%	100%	–	10%	8%	15%	Ecuador
94%	100%	42%	56%	36%	2%	Egypt
96%	98%	51%	24%	27%	10%	El Salvador
–	–	4%	26%	10%	5%	Equatorial Guinea
48%	59%	13%	60%	–	15%	Eritrea
93%	95%	53%	–	–	18%	Estonia
30%	55%	19%	67%	54%	8%	Ethiopia
100%	100%	–	9%	6%	6%	Fiji
99%	98%	53%	1%	–	37%	Finland
100%	100%	55%	1%	–	11%	France
–	–	–	38%	26%	–	Gabon
67%	87%	36%	70%	47%	–	Gambia
88%	89%	53%	–	–	7%	Georgia
100%	100%	43%	1%	–	32%	Germany
74%	84%	22%	39%	24%	9%	Ghana
93%	93%	48%	4%	–	9%	Greece
82%	93%	–	39%	38%	9%	Guatemala
41%	68%	11%	73%	50%	9%	Guinea
45%	79%	–	79%	32%	8%	Guinea-Bissau
96%	97%	58%	2%	1%	20%	Guyana
46%	49%	–	54%	52%	4%	Haiti
100%	100%	42%	28%	27%	9%	Honduras
100%	100%	53%	1%	–	8%	Hungary
98%	98%	58%	1%	–	35%	Iceland
90%	100%	36%	58%	34%	9%	India
100%	100%	31%	18%	10%	8%	Indonesia
95%	100%	35%	30%	–	3%	Iran
78%	92%	–	–	29%	8%	Iraq
100%	100%	52%	1%	–	12%	Ireland
96%	100%	55%	6%	–	13%	Israel
100%	100%	54%	2%	–	10%	Italy
99%	100%	38%	9%	19%	13%	Jamaica
100%	100%	44%	1%	–	7%	Japan
95%	94%	42%	16%	7%	1%	Jordan
98%	97%	53%	–	–	10%	Kazakhstan
85%	85%	28%	24%	14%	4%	Kenya
–	–	–	–	–	20%	Korea (North)
95%	94%	32%	4%	1%	6%	Korea (South)

. *The World's Women 2000: Trends and Statistics.* NY, 2000 (**Cols 3, 4, 5 and 6**); UNESCO. *Statistical Yearbook 1999* (**Cols 5, 6 and 7**); UNIFEM. *Progress of the World's Women.* 2000 Report (**Col 7**)

School, Work, Power

Countries	1 Gender Development Index country rank 2000	2 The Vote Date of women's suffrage on equal terms with men	3 Women Working % of women who are economically active 1999	4 Workplaces late 1990s % of economically active women working in:		
				agriculture	industry	services
Kuwait	44	no women vote	41%	–	–	–
Kyrgyzstan	–	1918	61%	48%	7%	38%
Laos	118	1958	75%	–	–	–
Latvia	46	1918	61%	18%	20%	62%
Lebanon	69	1952	29%	–	–	–
Lesotho	111	1965	47%	–	–	–
Liberia	–	1946	–	–	–	–
Libya	61	1963	25%	–	–	–
Lithuania	42	1918	58%	18%	21%	61%
Luxembourg	19	1919	38%	2%	7%	91%
Macedonia	–	1946	50%	6%	41%	51%
Madagascar	123	1959	69%	–	–	–
Malawi	137	1964	78%	–	–	–
Malaysia	54	1957	48%	14%	30%	56%
Maldives	68	1932	66%	–	–	–
Mali	138	1956	72%	–	–	–
Mauritania	127	1961	63%	–	–	–
Mauritius	59	1956	38%	13%	43%	45%
Mexico	49	1953	39%	13%	19%	68%
Moldova	86	1917	60%	51%	9%	38%
Mongolia	95	1924	73%	–	–	–
Morocco	102	1959	41%	–	–	–
Mozambique	144	1975	83%	–	–	–
Namibia	101	1989	54%	–	–	–
Nepal	119	1951	57%	–	–	–
Netherlands	9	1919	45%	2%	9%	85%
New Zealand	18	1893	57%	6%	13%	81%
Nicaragua	97	1955	47%	–	–	–
Niger	146	1956	70%	–	–	–
Nigeria	124	1978	48%	–	–	–
Norway	3	1913	59%	2%	10%	87%
Oman	78	1996	19%	–	–	–
Pakistan	120	1956	35%	67%	11%	22%
Panama	51	1946	43%	3%	11%	86%
Papua New Guinea	110	1975	67%	–	–	–
Paraguay	75	1961	37%	1%	13%	87%
Peru	73	1979	34%	5%	12%	83%
Philippines	63	1937	49%	28%	13%	59%
Poland	36	1918	57%	20%	21%	59%
Portugal	28	1975	51%	16%	25%	60%
Qatar	48	1999	36%	–	–	–
Romania	55	1946	51%	43%	24%	33%

Sources: UNDP. *Human Development Report 2002* (**Cols 1, 3, 4, 5, 7 and 8**); Inter-Parliamentary Union (**Col 2**); Economic Commission for Europ *Women and Men in Europe and North America*, 2000 (**Cols 3 & 4**) FAO. *GenderFacts*, 2002 (**Col 4**);

5 School enrolled in primary school 1999 or latest available data		6 University Women as a % of students 2000 or most recent available	7 Literacy 2000		8 Government Women as a % of elected officials 2002	Countries
girls	boys		% of women who are illiterate	% of men who are illiterate		
77%	78%	67%	20%	18%	0%	Kuwait
100%	100%	52%	–	–	10%	Kyrgyzstan
100%	100%	33%	50%	31%	21%	Laos
93%	98%	60%	1%	–	17%	Latvia
100%	100%	49%	20%	5%	2%	Lebanon
100%	100%	60%	6%	19%	4%	Lesotho
–	61%	–	63%	46%	8%	Liberia
100%	100%	46%	32%	12%	–	Libya
96%	99%	56%	1%	–	11%	Lithuania
100%	87%	–	1%	–	17%	Luxembourg
98%	100%	55%	–	–	7%	Macedonia
91%	92%	46%	41%	–	8%	Madagascar
100%	100%	25%	53%	28%	9%	Malawi
100%	100%	–	16%	11%	10%	Malaysia
100%	100%	–	4%	7%	6%	Maldives
40%	58%	20%	67%	61%	12%	Mali
75%	84%	18%	71%	50%	–	Mauritania
100%	100%	47%	19%	13%	6%	Mauritius
100%	100%	48%	11%	8%	16%	Mexico
97%	98%	54%	2%	–	13%	Moldova
91%	86%	60%	1%	11%	11%	Mongolia
74%	97%	41%	64%	43%	1%	Morocco
50%	70%	24%	72%	42%	30%	Mozambique
100%	100%	61%	19%	–	25%	Namibia
96%	100%	24%	76%	59%	6%	Nepal
100%	100%	48%	1%	–	36%	Netherlands
100%	100%	57%	1%	–	31%	New Zealand
100%	100%	54%	36%	35%	21%	Nicaragua
23%	36%	–	92%	79%	1%	Niger
87%	100%	–	44%	33%	3%	Nigeria
100%	100%	56%	–	–	36%	Norway
74%	78%	51%	38%	–	–	Oman
42%	87%	–	72%	50%	–	Pakistan
100%	100%	60%	9%	9%	10%	Panama
74%	87%	25%	32%	19%	2%	Papua New Guinea
100%	100%	51%	8%	6%	3%	Paraguay
100%	100%	–	15%	5%	18%	Peru
100%	100%	57%	5%	5%	18%	Philippines
95%	97%	57%	1%	–	20%	Poland
100%	100%	56%	10%	–	19%	Portugal
86%	87%	73%	17%	21%	–	Qatar
100%	100%	50%	3%	–	11%	Romania

N. *The World's Women 2000: Trends and Statistics*. NY, 2000 (**Cols 3, 4, 5 and 6**); UNESCO. *Statistical Yearbook 1999* (**Cols 5, 6 and 7**); UNIFEM. *ogress of the World's Women*. 2000 Report (**Col 7**)

School, Work, Power

Countries	1 Gender Development Index country rank 2000	2 The Vote Date of women's suffrage on equal terms with men	3 Women Working % of women who are economically active 1999	4 Workplaces late 1990s % of economically active women working in:		
				agriculture	industry	services
Russia	52	1917	59%	7%	10%	84%
Rwanda	135	1961	83%	–	–	–
Samoa	–	1990	–	–	–	–
Saudi Arabia	72	no one votes	21%	–	–	–
Senegal	130	1956	61%	–	–	–
Seychelles	–	1948	–	–	–	–
Sierra Leone	–	1961	44%	–	–	–
Singapore	24	1957	50%	–	25%	75%
Slovakia	34	1920	63%	6%	27%	67%
Slovenia	27	1945	54%	13%	31%	57%
Solomon Islands	69.7	1974	–	–	–	–
Somalia	–	1958	–	–	–	–
South Africa	88	1994	46%	–	–	–
Spain	21	1931	37%	6%	14%	80%
Sri Lanka	70	1931	42%	40%	24%	34%
Sudan	116	1965	34%	–	–	–
Suriname	–	1953	36%	2%	6%	90%
Swaziland	103	1968	42%	–	–	–
Sweden	4	1919	63%	1%	12%	87%
Switzerland	14	1971	52%	4%	15%	82%
Syria	92	1953	28%	–	–	–
Tajikistan	94 .	1924	57%	–	–	–
Tanzania	126	1959	82%	–	–	–
Thailand	60	1932	73%	51%	17%	32%
Togo	117	1956	54%	–	–	–
Trinidad & Tobago	45	1946	44%	5%	13%	82%
Tunisia	81	1959	37%	20%	–	–
Turkey	71	1930	49%	65%	13%	21%
Turkmenistan	–	1927	62%	–	–	–
Uganda	125	1962	80%	–	–	–
Ukraine	66	1919	55%	–	–	–
United Arab Emirates	47	no one votes	32%	–	–	–
United Kingdom	10	1928	53%	1%	13%	86%
United States of America	6	1920	58%	1%	13%	85%
Uruguay	37	1932	48%	2%	17%	82%
Uzbekistan	76	1938	62%	–	–	–
Venezuela	57	1946	43%	2%	14%	84%
Vietnam	89	1946	74%	71%	9%	20%
Yemen	128	1967	30%	–	–	–
Yugoslavia	–	1946	–	–	–	–
Zambia	129	1964	65%	–	–	–
Zimbabwe	107	1957	67%	38%	10%	52%

Sources: UNDP. *Human Development Report 2002* (**Cols 1, 3, 4, 5, 7 and 8**); Inter-Parliamentary Union (**Col 2**); Economic Commission for Europe *Women and Men in Europe and North America*, 2000 (**Cols 3 & 4**) FAO. *GenderFacts*, 2002 (**Col 4**);

5 School enrolled in primary school 999 or latest available data		6 University Women as a % of students 2000 or most recent available	7 Literacy 2000		8 Government Women as a % of elected officials 2002	Countries
girls	boys		% of women who are illiterate	% of men who are illiterate		
100%	100%	53%	1%	–	8%	Russia
80%	82%	–	40%	30%	26%	Rwanda
100%	100%	–	–	–	6%	Samoa
75%	77%	47%	33%	28%	–	Saudi Arabia
65%	78%	–	72%	57%	17%	Senegal
–	–	–	–	–	24%	Seychelles
41%	60%	–	77%	55%	9%	Sierra Leone
93%	95%	46%	12%	4%	12%	Singapore
–	100%	49%	–	–	14%	Slovakia
98%	98%	57%	1%	–	12%	Slovenia
89%	100%	–	–	–	0%	Solomon Islands
–	18%	–	–	–	–	Somalia
100%	100%	48%	16%	18%	30%	South Africa
100%	100%	53%	3%	–	28%	Spain
100%	100%	44%	11%	7%	–	Sri Lanka
47%	55%	–	54%	42%	10%	Sudan
–	–	53%	7%	5%	18%	Suriname
100%	100%	52%	21%	22%	3%	Swaziland
100%	100%	56%	1%	–	43%	Sweden
–	–	38%	1%	–	23%	Switzerland
96%	100%	39%	40%	14%	10%	Syria
94%	96%	26%	1%	–	13%	Tajikistan
66%	67%	20%	33%	21%	22%	Tanzania
96%	98%	53%	6%	4%	9%	Thailand
99%	100%	17%	57%	33%	5%	Togo
98%	99%	55%	3%	1%	17%	Trinidad & Tobago
100%	100%	45%	40%	21%	12%	Tunisia
100%	100%	35%	23%	8%	4%	Turkey
–	–	–	–	–	26%	Turkmenistan
68%	81%	37%	43%	26%	25%	Uganda
86%	87%	51%	1%	–	8%	Ukraine
87%	91%	72%	21%	21%	0%	United Arab Emirates
100%	100%	50%	1%	–	18%	United Kingdom
100%	100%	56%	1%	–	14%	United States of America
100%	100%	–	2%	3%	12%	Uruguay
76%	79%	–	16%	–	7%	Uzbekistan
93%	90%	–	7%	8%	10%	Venezuela
100%	100%	–	9%	4%	26%	Vietnam
40%	100%	13%	75%	–	1%	Yemen
70%	69%	55%	–	–	7%	Yugoslavia
86%	91%	30%	29%	14%	12%	Zambia
100%	100%	29%	10%	10%	10%	Zimbabwe

N. The World's Women 2000: Trends and Statistics. NY, 2000 (**Cols 3, 4, 5 and 6**); UNESCO. Statistical Yearbook 1999 (**Cols 5, 6 and 7**); UNIFEM.
'ogress of the World's Women. 2000 Report (**Col 7**)

Sources

PART 1 WOMEN IN THE WORLD

1 THE STATE OF WOMEN

UNDP. *Human Development Report 2001*. New York and Oxford: Oxford University Press, 2001

Population Reference Bureau. *Women of Our World 2002*. Washington DC: PRB, 2002

2 IN THEIR PLACE

US State Department. *Country Human Rights Practices, 2000*, 2001

Mahnaz Afkhami, ed. Faith and Freedom. *Women's Human Rights in the Muslim World*. Syrause: Syracuse University Press, 1995

Gita Sahgal & Nira Yuval-Davis, eds. *Refusing Holy Orders: Women and Fundamentalism in Britain*. London: Virago, 1992

Women Against Fundamentalism Journal. London, various issues

Press reports

3 STATES AGAINST DISCRIMINATION

<www.un.org/womenwatch/daw/cedaw/states.htm>

PART 2 FAMILIES

4 HOUSEHOLDS

US Bureau of the Census

Economic Commission for Europe. *Women & Men in Europe & North America*. NY and Geneva: United Nations, 2000

UN. *The World's Women 2000: Trends and Statistics*. NY, 2000

UN Center for Human Settlements, various reports

Suzanne Bianchi & Lynne Casper. *American Families*. PRB Population Bulletin, December 2000

5 MARRIAGE AND DIVORCE

UN Department of Economic & Social Affairs. *World Marriage Patterns 2000*

UNICEF. *Early Marriage/Child Spouses*. Innocenti Digest #7, March 2001

Center for Reproductive Law & Policy. *Reproductive Rights 2000*. NY: CLRP, 2000

UN. *The World's Women 2000: Trends and Statistics*. NY, 2000

Divorce Magazine.Com

US Census Bureau/Economic Commission for Europe. *Women and Men in Europe and North America*, 2000

6 LESBIANS

Amnesty International. *Breaking the Silence: Human Rights Violations Based on Sexual Orientation*. NY: Amnesty International, 1994

Rachel Rosenbloom, ed. *Unspoken Rules: Sexual Orientation and Women's Human Rights*. USA: International Gay and Lesbian Human Rights Commission, 1995

International Lesbian and Gay Association. *Fourth Annual Report*, 2000

<www.actwin.com/eatonohio/gay/GAY.htm>

K6 Alliance for Gay Secession and Liberation

Partners Task Force for Gay and Lesbian Couples: <www.buddybuddy.com>

International Gay and Lesbian Human Rights Commission (IGLHRC). various publications

US Department of Justice. *Sourcebook of criminal justice statistics*, 2001

7 DOMESTIC VIOLENCE

UN Inter-Agency Campaign on Women's Human Rights in Latin America and the Caribbean

Human Rights Watch, various reports

UNFPA, various reports

World Organisation Against Torture. *Violence Against Women: 10 Reports/Year 2001*. Geneva: 2002

UN. *The World's Women 2000: Trends and Statistics*. NY, 2000

UNICEF. *Domestic Violence Against Women and Girls*, 2000

Demographic and Health Survey, various country reports

USA, Dept of Justice. *Sourcebook of Criminal Justice Statistics*, 2001

<www.endvaw.org>

World Health Organization, Database on Violence Against Women

European Women's Lobby. *Unveiling the hidden data on domestic violence in the European Union*, 2000

Population Reports. *Ending Violence Against Women*. December 1999

Center for Disease Control (USA). *National Vital Statistics Report*. October 2001

UNFPA. *State of the World 2000*

USAID/Office of Women in Development. Violence Against Women. *Newsletter, Summer 1997*. Washington DC

WHO. *Violence Against Women and HIV/AIDS*, 2000

WHO. *Violence Against Women Living in Situations of Armed Conflict*, 2000

Bunch, Charlotte, and Roxanna Carrillo, *Gender Violence: A Development and Human Rights Issue*. New Brunswick, NJ: Center for Women's Global Leadership, 1991

News reports

8 MURDER

World Health Organization, Database on Violence Against Women

UN. *The World's Women 2000: Trends and Statistics*. NY, 2000

UNICEF. *Domestic Violence Against Women and Girls*, 2000

Demographic and Health Survey, various country reports

USA, Dept of Justice. *Sourcebook of Criminal Justice Statistics*, 2001

News sources

PART 3 BIRTHRIGHTS

9 MOTHERHOOD

Alan Guttmacher Institute. *Sharing Responsibility: Women, Society & Abortion Worldwide*, 2001

Population Reference Bureau. *The World's Youth 2000*. Washington DC: 2000

UN. *The World's Women 2000: Trends and Statistics*. NY, 2000

UNDP. *Human Development Report 2001*. New York and Oxford: Oxford University Press, 2001

10 CONTRACEPTION

Center for Reproductive Law & Policy. *Emergency Contraception: An analysis of laws and polices around the world*. 2000.

Population Reference Bureau. *2001 World Population Data Sheet*. Washington DC: PRB, 2001

UN Economic and Social Commission for Asia & The Pacific. *Statistics on Women in Asia & The Pacific*. 1999

UNFPA. *The State of World Population 2001*

Consortium for Emergency Contraception, New York

11 ABORTION

Center for Reproductive Law and Policy (NY). *The World's Abortion Laws 2000*

UN. Economic & Social Development/Population Division. *Abortion Policies: A Global Review*, 2001

Alan Guttmacher Institute. *Sharing Responsibility: Women, Society & Abortion Worldwide*, 2001

NARAL. *Who Decides? A state by state review of abortion and reproductive rights 2002*. NY: 2002

National Abortion Federation. *Violence and Disruption Statistics*, 2002

UN. *The World's Women 2000: Trends and Statistics*. NY, 2000

World Health Organization. *Unsafe Abortion: Global and regional estimates of mortality due to unsafe abortion*. 1997

12 MATERNAL MORTALITY

Centers for Disease Control, USA, various reports

UNFPA. *The State of the World Population 2001*

UNDP. *Human Development Report 2001*. New York and Oxford: Oxford University Press, 2001

UNICEF. *State of the World's Children, 2002*

UN. *The World's Women 2000: Trends and Statistics*. NY, 2000

UNICEF. *State of World's Children, 2000*

Ann Tinker & Marjorie Koblinsky. *Making Motherhood Safe*. World Bank, 1993

13 SON PREFERENCE

Census of India 2001
   <www.censusindia.net/results/provindia2.html>

China Statistical Yearbook 2000

UNDP. *Korea Human Development Report 1998*

US Census Bureau. *Son Preference in Asia – Report of a Symposium*, 2001 (the "International Symposium on Issues Related to Sex Preference for Children in the Rapidly Changing Demographic Dynamics in Asia" was held in Seoul, South Korea, in November 1994)

Koh Eng Chuan. Sex selection at birth. *Statistics Singapore Newsletter* V 17 #3, January 1995

A. J. Coale. Excess female mortality and the balance of the sexes. *Population Development Review* 1991

UN. *The World's Women 2000: Trends and Statistics*. NY, 2000

Elisabeth Croll. *Endangered Daughters: Discrimination and Development in Asia*. Routledge: 2000

14 POPULATION POLICIES

UNFPA. *The State of World Population 2001*

UNFPA. *Financial Resource Flows for Population Activities in 1999*, 2000

Population Reference Bureau. *2001 World Population Data Sheet*, 2001

PART 4 BODY POLITICS

15 BREAST CANCER

International Agency for Research on Cancer/World Health Organization. *Globocan 2000: Cancer Incidence, Mortality, and Prevalence Worldwide,* 2001

American Cancer Society. *Breast Cancer Facts & Figures 2001–2002*, 2002

16 HIV/AIDS

Centers for Disease Control (US). *HIV/AIDS Surveillance and Epidemiology 2000*

UNAIDS. *AIDS Epidemic Update 2001.*

UNFPA. *The State of the World's Population 2001*

World Health Organization. *Weekly Epidemiological Record*, 76 # 49 & 50, 2001

UNAIDS. *Table of country-specific HIV/AIDS estimates and data end 2001,* 2002

17 SPORTS

Australian Sports Commission.
   <www.activeaustralia.org/women>

International Olympic Committee

18 BEAUTY

<www.missuniverse.com>

Global Beauties <www.globalbeauties.com>

<www.avoncompany.com/world>

American Society for Aesthetic Plastic Surgery

Pamela Sauer, "A Makeover of Global Proportions", *Chemical Market Reporter* Dec 2001

News reports

19 UNDER THE KNIFE

World Health organization. Women's Health
   <www.who.int/frh-whd/FGM/>

CRLP. *Female Circumcision/Female Genital Mutilation (FC/FGM): Global Laws and Policies Towards Elimination*. NY, 2001

Population Reference Bureau. *Youth in Sub-Saharan Africa.* Washington DC, 2001

Population Reference Bureau. *Abandoning Female Genital Cutting: Prevalence, Attitudes, and Efforts to end the Practice.* Washington DC: 2001

UN. *The World's Women 2000: Trends and Statistics.* NY, 2000

World Health Organization. *Female genital mutilation: An overview.* Geneva, 1998

20 THE GLOBAL SEX TRADE

Donna Hughes, Laura Joy Sporcic, Z. Mendelsohn, Vanessa Chirgwin. *The Factbook on Global Sexual Exploitation.* Coalition Against Trafficking in Women, 1999

Lin Lean Lim, ed. *The Sex Sector: The economic and social bases of prostitution in Southeast Asia.* Geneva: International Labour Office, 1998

US AID. *Trafficking in Persons: USAID's Response,* September 2001

Kvinnoforum. *A Resource Book for Working Against Trafficking in Women and Girls*

Baltic Sea Region. Stockholm, 2002

US Department of State. *Trafficking in Persons Report*, June 2002

US Congressional Research Service. *Trafficking in Women and Children,* May 2000

US Immigration and Naturalization Service. *The Mail-Order Bride Industry and Its Impact on US Immigration*, 2001

21 RAPE

UN Inter-Agency Campaign on Women's Human Rights in Latin America and the Caribbean

Human Rights Watch, various reports

World Organisation Against Torture. *Violence Against Women: 10 Reports/Year 2001.* Geneva: 2002

UNICEF. *Domestic Violence Against Women and Girls,* 2000

Demographic and Health Survey, various country reports

UN. *International Crime Victimization Survey*, 2001

USA, Dept of Justice. *Sourcebook of Criminal Justice Statistics*, 2001

End Violence Against Women <www.endvaw.org>

World Health Organization, Database on Violence Against Women

European Women's Lobby. *Unveiling the hidden data on domestic violence in the European Union*, 2000

Population Reports. *Ending Violence Against Women*, December 1999

WHO. *Violence Against Women and HIV/AIDS*, 2000

WHO. *Violence Against Women Living in Situations of Armed Conflict,* 2000

South Africa Survey 2000/2001

Elizabeth Shrader. *Methodologies to measure the gender dimensions of crime and violence.* World Bank 2000

UN. *World Crime Survey, Sixth Survey*, 2000

PART 5 WORK

22 WORKING FOR WAGES

Economic Commission for Europe. *Women and Men in Europe and North America,* 2000.

UN. *The World's Women 2000: Trends and Statistics.* NY, 2000

UNDP. *Human Development Report 2001.* New York and Oxford: Oxford University Press, 2001

23 WORKPLACES

Economic Commission for Europe. *Women and Men in Europe and North America,* 2000.

UN. *The World's Women 2000: Trends and Statistics.* NY, 2000

UNDP. *Human Development Report 2001.* New York and Oxford: Oxford University Press, 2001

24 UNEQUAL OPPORTUNITIES

Economic Commission for Europe. *Women and Men in Europe and North America,* 2000

Human Rights Watch. *From the Household to the Factory: Sex Discrimination in the Guatemala Labor Force.* NY: HRW, 2002

Sylvia Chant & Cathy McIlwaine. *Women of a Lesser Cost.* London: Pluto, 1995

UN. *1999 World Survey on the Role of Women in Development*

UN. *The World's Women 2000: Trends and Statistics.* NY, 2000

UNDP. *Human Development Report 2001.* New York and Oxford: Oxford University Press, 2001

South African Institute of Race Relations. *South Africa Survey 2000/2001.* Johannesburg, 2001

25 FIELDWORK

Susan Bullock. *Women and Work.* London: Zed Books, 1994

United Nations Development Programme. *Human Development Report, 1995.* New York: Oxford University Press, 1995

United States Agency for International Development. *Women in Development: A Report to Congress by the United States Agency for International Development.* Washington DC: Government Printing Office, 1990.

UNDP. *Human Development Report 2001.* New York and Oxford: Oxford University Press, 2001

UN. *The World's Women 2000: Trends and Statistics.* NY, 2000

FAO. *GenderFacts,* 2002

Economic Commission for Europe. *Women and Men in Europe and North America,* 2000

26 UNPAID WORK

Economic Commission for Europe. *Women and Men in Europe and North America,* 2000

UN. *The World's Women 2000: Trends and Statistics.* NY, 2000

University of Michigan, Institute for Social Research, 2001, various reports

27 MIGRATION

ILO. *International Labor Migration Database*

Heyzer, Noleen, et al. *The Trade in Domestic Workers.* London: Zed, 1994

Sylvia Chant. *Gender and Migration in Developing Countries.* London: Belhaven Press, 1992

UN. *International Migration Policies and the Status of Female Migrants.* NY: UN, 1995

UN/INSTRAW. *The Migration of Women.* Santo Domingo: INSTRAW, 1994

Peter Stalker. *The Work of Strangers: A survey of international labour migration.* Geneva: ILO, 1994

Peter Stalker. *Workers without Frontiers.* ILO/Lynne Reiner Press, 2000

UN. *Women in a Changing Global Economy.* NY: UN 1995

Saira Shameem & Elizabeth Brady. *Understanding International Migration.* APIM, 1998

PART 6 TO HAVE AND HAVE NOT

28 LITERACY

Nancy Hafkin & Nancy Taggart. *Gender, Information Technology and Developing Countries: An Analytic Study*, USAID/Office of Women in Development, June 2001

UNIFEM. *Progress of the World's Women. 2000 Report*, 2000

UNESCO. *Statistical Yearbook, 1999*, 1999

UNDP. *Human Development Report, 2001.* New York and Oxford: Oxford University Press, 2001

Mileno Pires & Catherine Scott, "East Timorese women" in Torben Retboll, ed., *East Timor: Occupation & Resistance.* International Working Group for Indigenous Affairs, Copenhagen, Denmark, 1998

29 SCHOOL

UNESCO. *Statistical Yearbook 1999*, 1999

UNDP. *Human Development Report 2001*, New York and Oxford: Oxford University Press, 2001

UN. *The World's Women 2000: Trends and Statistics.* NY, 2000

30 HIGHER EDUCATION

UNESCO. *Statistical Yearbook 1999*, 1999

UN. *The World's Women 2000: Trends and Statistics.* NY, 2000

American Council on Education. Fact Sheet on Higher Education, 2001

31 WIRED WOMEN

Nancy Hafkin & Nancy Taggart. *Gender, Information Technology and Developing Countries: An Analytic Study.* USAID/Office of Women in Development, June 2001

NUA Internet Surveys. <www.nua.com>

Cyberatlas: <cyberatlas.internet.com>

US Department of Commerce. *Falling Through the Net*, 2000

32 PROPERTY

US Bureau of the Census, various reports;

American Housing Survey

US State Department. *Country Report on Human Rights Practices 2001*, 2001

FAO. *World Agricultural Census*, 2001

FAO. *Rural women's access to land in Latin America*, 2001

33 POVERTY

CIA. *World Factbook*, 2001

World Bank, various reports

US Bureau of the Census

UN, Department of Economic & Social Affairs, "Millennium Indicators"

State of the Microcredit Summit Campaign 2001 <www.microcreditsummit.org/SOCReport2001.doc>

UNIFEM. *Progress of the World's Women 2000.* NY: UN, 2000

Population Reference Bureau. *Kids Count Datasheet 2000*

UNICEF. *A League Table of Child Poverty in Rich Countries*, June 2000

UNFPA. *State of the World's Population 2001*

UNDP. *Human Development Report 2001*, New York and Oxford: Oxford University Press, 2001

EUROSTAT. *The Social Situation in the European Union 2002*, 2002

34 DEBT

UNICEF. *The Progress of Nations 1999*, 2000

World Bank. various reports

International Monetary Fund, various reports

UNDP. *Human Development Report 2001*, New York and Oxford: Oxford University Press, 2001

PART 7 POWER

35 THE VOTE

Inter-Parliamentary Union

News reports

Sumiko Iwao. *The Japanese Woman.* Cambridge: Harvard University Press, 1993

Caroline Daley & Melanie Nolan. *Suffrage & Beyond: International Feminist Perspectives.* NY: NYU Press, 1994

Irene Franck & David Brownstone. *Women's World: A Timeline of Women in History.* NY: Harper, 1995

36 WOMEN IN GOVERNMENT

Inter-Parliamentary Union, various reports

East Timor Institute for Reconstruction Monitoring and Analysis

US State Department, various reports

UNDP, *Human Development Report 2001.* New York and Oxford: Oxford University Press, 2001

37 SEATS OF POWER

Islamic Republic of Iran Management and Planning Organization. *Socio-Economic Characteristics of Women in Iran*, Tehran, 2001

Mala N. Htun. Women's Leadership in Latin America: Trends & Challenges, In *Politics Matter: A Dialogue of Women Political Leaders*, 2000

The Inter-Parliamentary Union

Gita Sen, quoted in UNIFEM. *Progress of the World's Women 2000*

UNESCO, *Country Reports on the state of women in urban local governments* 2001
  <www.unescap.org/huset/women/reports/index.htm>
Council of European Municipalities and Regions, "Women in Local Politics in the EU", 2000

38 CRISIS ZONES

WHO. *Violence Against Women Living in Situations of Armed Conflict,* 2000
Human Rights Watch, various reports
World Organisation Against Torture. *Violence Against Women: 10 Reports/Year 2001.* Geneva, 2002
US Committee for Refugees, various reports
UN High Commission for Refugees, various reports
News reports

39 WOMEN IN THE MILITARY

Committee on Women in NATO Forces, Brussels, Belgium
ISSP. *The Military Balance 2001–2002.* London: ISSP, 2001
Center for the Study of Sexual Minorities in the Military, California
Mazurana, Dyan with Eugenia Piza-Lopez. *Gender Mainstreaming in Peace Support Operations: Moving Beyond Rhetoric to Practice*. London: International Alert, 2002

40 FEMINIST ORGANIZING

News reports

Index

Page numbers in **bold** indicate that a reference is made in a map or graphic. Countries have been indexed only if they are mentioned in the main text or in text on a map, or if they are included in a graphic.